HATTIN

GREAT BATTLES

# HATTIN

JOHN FRANCE

OXFORD
UNIVERSITY PRESS

# OXFORD
## UNIVERSITY PRESS

Great Clarendon Street, Oxford, OX2 6DP,
United Kingdom

Oxford University Press is a department of the University of Oxford.
It furthers the University's objective of excellence in research, scholarship,
and education by publishing worldwide. Oxford is a registered trade mark of
Oxford University Press in the UK and in certain other countries

Published in the United States of America by Oxford University Press
198 Madison Avenue, New York, NY 10016, United States of America

British Library Cataloguing in Publication Data
Data available

Library of Congress Control Number: 2015940146

ISBN 978–0–19–964695–1

Printed in Great Britain by
Clays Ltd, St Ives plc

*To the West Point Class of 2012*

# FOREWORD

For those who practise war in the twenty-first century the idea of a 'great battle' can seem no more than the echo of a remote past. The names on regimental colours or the events commemorated at mess dinners bear little relationship to patrolling in dusty villages or waging 'wars amongst the people'. Contemporary military doctrine downplays the idea of victory, arguing that wars end by negotiation not by the smashing of an enemy army or navy. Indeed it erodes the very division between war and peace, and with it the aspiration to fight a culminating 'great battle'.

And yet to take battle out of war is to redefine war, possibly to the point where some would argue that it ceases to be war. Carl von Clausewitz, who experienced two 'great battles' at first hand—Jena in 1806 and Borodino in 1812—wrote in *On War* that major battle is 'concentrated war', and 'the centre of gravity of the entire campaign'. Clausewitz's remarks related to the theory of strategy. He recognized that in practice armies might avoid battles, but even then the efficacy of their actions relied on the latent threat of fighting. Winston Churchill saw the importance of battles in different terms, not for their place within war but for their impact on historical and national narratives. His forebear, the Duke of Marlborough, commanded in four major battles and named his palace after the most famous of them, Blenheim, fought in 1704. Battles, Churchill wrote in his life of Marlborough, are 'the principal milestones in secular history'. For him, 'Great battles, won or lost, change the entire course of events, create new standards of values, new moods, new atmospheres, in armies and nations, to which all must conform'.

Clausewitz's experience of war was shaped by Napoleon. Like Marlborough, the French emperor sought to bring his enemies to battle. However, each lived within a century of the other, and they fought their wars in the same continent and even on occasion on adjacent ground. Winston Churchill's own experience of war, which spanned the late nineteenth-century colonial conflicts of the British Empire as well as two world wars, became increasingly distanced from the sorts of battle he and Clausewitz described. In 1898 Churchill rode in a cavalry charge in a battle which crushed the Madhist forces of the Sudan in a single day. Four years later the British commander at Omdurman, Lord Kitchener, brought the South African War to a conclusion after a two-year guerrilla conflict in which no climactic battle occurred. Both Churchill and Kitchener served as British Cabinet ministers in the First World War, a conflict in which battles lasted weeks, and even months, and which, despite their scale and duration, did not produce clear-cut outcomes. The 'Battle' of Verdun ran for all but one month of 1916 and that of the Somme for five months. The potentially decisive naval action at Jutland spanned a more traditional twenty-four-hour timetable but was not conclusive and was not replicated during the war. In the Second World War, the major struggle in waters adjacent to Europe, the 'Battle' of the Atlantic, was fought from 1940 to early 1944.

Clausewitz would have called these twentieth-century 'battles' campaigns, or even seen them as wars in their own right. The determination to seek battle and to venerate its effects may therefore be culturally determined, the product of time and place, rather than an inherent attribute of war. The ancient historian Victor Davis Hanson has argued that seeking battle is a 'western way of war' derived from classical Greece. Seemingly supportive of his argument are the writings of Sun Tzu, who flourished in warring states in China between two and five centuries before the birth of Christ, and who pointed out that the most effective way of waging war was to avoid the risks and dangers of actual fighting. Hanson has provoked strong criticism: those who argue that wars can be won without battles are not only to be found in Asia. Eighteenth-century European commanders, deploying armies in close-order formations in order to deliver concentrated fires, realized that the destructive consequences of battle for their own troops could be self-defeating. After the First World War, Basil Liddell Hart developed a theory of strategy which he called 'the indirect approach', and suggested that manoeuvre might substitute for hard fighting, even if its success still relied on the inherent threat of battle.

The winners of battles have been celebrated as heroes, and nations have used their triumphs to establish their founding myths. It is precisely for these reasons that their legacies have outlived their direct political consequences. Commemorated in painting, verse, and music, marked by monumental memorials, and used as the way points for the periodization of history, they have enjoyed cultural afterlives. These are evident in many capitals, in place names and statues, not least in Paris and London. The French tourist who finds himself in a London taxi travelling from Trafalgar Square to Waterloo Station should reflect on his or her own domestic peregrinations from the Rue de Rivoli to the Gare d'Austerlitz. Today's Mongolia venerates the memory of Genghis Khan while Greece and Macedonia scrap over the rights to Alexander the Great.

This series of books on 'great battles' tips its hat to both Clausewitz and Churchill. Each of its volumes situates the battle which it discusses in the context of the war in which it occurred, but each then goes on to discuss its legacy, its historical interpretation and reinterpretation, its place in national memory and commemoration, and its manifestations in art and culture. These are not easy books to write. The victors were more often celebrated than the defeated; the effect of loss on the battlefield could be cultural oblivion. However, that point is not universally true: the British have done more over time to mark their defeats at Gallipoli in 1915 and Dunkirk in 1940 than their conquerors on both occasions. For the history of war to thrive and be productive it needs to embrace the view from 'the other side of the hill', to use the Duke of Wellington's words. The battle the British call Omdurman is for the Sudanese the Battle of Kerreri; the Germans called Waterloo 'la Belle Alliance' and Jutland Skagerrak. Indeed the naming of battles could itself be a sign not only of geographical precision or imprecision (Kerreri is more accurate but as a hill rather than a town is harder to find on a small-scale map), but also of cultural choice. In 1914 the German general staff opted to name their defeat of the Russians in East Prussia not Allenstein (as geography suggested) but Tannenberg, in order to claim revenge for the defeat of the Teutonic Knights in 1410.

Military history, more than many other forms of history, is bound up with national stories. All too frequently it fails to be comparative, to recognize that war is a 'clash of wills' (to quote Clausewitz once more), and so omits to address both parties to the fight. Cultural difference and, even more, linguistic ignorance can prevent the historian considering a battle in the round; so too can the availability of sources. Levels of literacy matter here, but so does cultural survival. Often these pressures can be congruent but they can also be divergent. Britain enjoys much higher levels of literacy than Afghanistan, but in 2002 the memory of the two countries' three wars flourished in the latter, thanks to an oral tradition, much more robustly than in the former, for whom literacy had created distance. And the historian who addresses cultural legacy is likely to face a much more challenging task the further in the past the battle occurred. The opportunity for invention and reinvention is simply greater the longer the lapse of time since the key event.

All historians of war must, nonetheless, never forget that, however rich and splendid the cultural legacy of a great battle, it was won and lost by fighting, by killing and being killed. The Battle of Waterloo has left as abundant a footprint as any, but the general who harvested most of its glory reflected on it in terms which have general applicability, and carry across time in their capacity to capture a universal truth. Wellington wrote to Lady Shelley in its immediate aftermath: 'I hope to God I have fought my last battle. It is a bad thing to be always fighting. While in the thick of it I am much too occupied to feel anything; but it is wretched just after. It is quite impossible to think of glory. Both mind and feelings are exhausted. I am wretched even at the moment of victory, and I always say that, next to a battle lost, the greatest misery is a battle gained.' Readers of this series should never forget the immediate suffering caused by battle, as well as the courage required to engage in it: the physical courage of the soldier, sailor, or warrior, and the moral courage of the commander, ready to hazard all on its uncertain outcomes.

HEW STRACHAN

# ACKNOWLEDGEMENTS

This book was begun in the academic year 2011–12 when I was the Charles Boal Ewing Visiting Professor at the United States Military Academy West Point. This was a remarkable and fulfilling experience and I would like to thank all the members of the History Department at West Point for their comradeship and support. I must especially express my gratitude to Colonel Lance Betros, the head of department during my tenure, and, of course, my friend Professor Clifford Rogers. It was an enormous privilege to be at West Point, above all because I had the opportunity to teach the cadets who upheld magnificently the traditions of the Academy.

This series was conceived by Professor Hew Strachan, Chichele Professor of the History of War at Oxford, and I must thank him for asking me to participate. I have profited immensely from discussion with other scholars, and above all I must acknowledge the lifelong help and support I have received from Professor Bernard Hamilton of the University of Nottingham. I owe a very great deal to Professor Kelly Devries of Loyola Baltimore, to Professor Tom Madden of St Louis University, to Professor Richard Abels of the United States Naval Academy at Annapolis, and to Professor B. S. Bachrach of Minneapolis University for sharing their knowledge of military history and the crusades so generously. Professor Jonathan Phillips of Royal Holloway has kindly fielded a number of questions for me. It has always been a pleasure to share the companionship and sharp intellect of Professor Jeremy Black of Exeter University. In Swansea, Professor Dan Power has been especially helpful, while I would like to thank Dr Martin Johnes and Dr Louise Miskell for their many kindnesses. I must also express my gratitude to Caroline Rauter and Jane Pressdee who were such excellent and patient librarians.

My wife, Angela France, generously worked through the manuscript correcting my English. Professor Peter Edbury of Cardiff University was extremely helpful on the sources for Hattin and the Third Crusade. Dr Michael Ehrlich of Bar Ilan University agreed to work through Chapter 2 and, through his intimate knowledge of Galilee, provided me with many excellent and helpful suggestions. Luciana O'Flaherty of Oxford University Press worked through the text and came up with numerous ideas to improve it. It must, however, be added that all errors and mistakes are mine, and not theirs.

JOHN FRANCE
*April 2015*

# CONTENTS

# LIST OF FIGURES

# LIST OF MAPS

# 1

# Salvation through Slaughter

A t the Battle of Hattin, on 3–4 July 1187, Saladin destroyed the army of the Latin kingdom of Jerusalem. Imad ad-Din, one of Saladin's secretaries who was present, described the gruesome consequences:

> The dead were scattered over the mountains and valleys, lying immobile on their sides. Hittin [Hattin] shrugged off their carcasses, and the perfume of victory was thick with the stench of them. I passed by them and saw the limbs of the fallen cast naked on the field of battle, scattered in pieces over the site of the encounter, lacerated and disjointed, with heads cracked open, throats split, spines broken, necks shattered, feet in pieces, noses mutilated, extremities torn off, members dismembered, parts shredded, eyes gouged out, stomachs disembowelled, hair coloured with blood, the praecordium [lower chest] slashed, fingers sliced off, the thorax shattered, the ribs broken, the joints dislocated, the chests smashed, throats slit, bodies cut in half, arms pulverised, lips shrivelled, foreheads pierced, forelocks dyed scarlet, breasts covered with blood, ribs pierced, elbows disjointed, bones broken, tunics torn off, faces lifeless, wounds gaping, skin flayed, fragments chopped off, hair lopped, backs skinless, bodies dismembered, teeth knocked out, blood spilt, life's last breath exhaled, necks lolling, joints slackened, pupils liquefied, heads hanging, livers crushed, ribs staved in, heads shattered, breasts flayed, spirits flown, their very ghosts crushed.

For Imad ad-Din this slaughter was entirely justifiable, because the victims were 'polytheists...impious enquirers after God'.[1] This was *jihad*, the Muslim form of holy war, and although it had different origins, it differed not at all in spirit from the crusade.

Eighty-eight years before, almost to the day, the First Crusade had shattered the forces of Islam and seized Jerusalem. This was the moment when the western Christian kingdom of Jerusalem was founded. A priest who was present in the army celebrated their victory in a similar style to Imad ad-Din:

> So let it suffice to say to say this much at least, that in the Temple and porch of Solomon, men rode in blood up to their knees and bridle reins. Indeed, it was a just and splendid judgement of God that this place should be filled with the blood of the unbelievers, since it had suffered so long from their blasphemies. The city was filled with corpses and blood.[2]

This is ideological warfare of a kind horribly familiar to the generations of the twentieth and twenty-first centuries. Since such hatred was at the root of what happened at Hattin, its genesis must be explored before we can understand the significance and consequences of the battle.

This was, on the face of it, a decisive battle. In 1099 the First Crusade had established a number of 'crusader states' in the Middle East, of which the most important was the kingdom of Jerusalem. One of the reasons for this success was the disunity of the local Islamic powers. However, gradually, powerful Muslim champions emerged who united large sections of the area and posed a threat to the very existence of these Latin Christian settlements. Saladin rose to be ruler of Egypt, Syria, and a vast empire beyond extending into modern Iraq, and in 1187 drew on the resources of these lands to create the army which won the Battle of Hattin. King Guy of Jerusalem had stripped all the garrisons of his realm in order to create a force capable of facing Saladin's attack. It was this field army which was destroyed at Hattin. The cities and castles of the kingdom were now virtually defenceless so that Saladin was able to capture almost all of them and thereby to destroy almost the entire kingdom of Jerusalem. The Holy City of Jerusalem, lost to the First Crusade in 1099, therefore, became once more a Muslim city.

Hattin is often seen as an inevitable victory: according to this view the First Crusade planted shallow foreign settlements in the Holy Land, and their presence provoked a growing spirit of *jihad*, Muslim holy war, which overwhelmed the settler states and their tiny European populations. But the truth is somewhat more complex. Many parts of the Middle East, especially those areas seized by the westerners, were not Muslim at all but eastern Christian: their populations often welcomed the new rulers. Within the lands conquered by the westerners some Muslims had little objection to the new government. Moreover, the self-styled champions of Islam were almost as strange to the peoples of the Middle East—Muslims and others—as the European crusaders. Since the middle of the eleventh century much of the Middle East had been dominated by Turks. They were a steppe people, very different from the predominantly Arab populations over whom they ruled as a narrow ruling elite sustained by their magnificent fighting soldiers. Saladin was a Kurd, a people from the very periphery of the settled lands of Islam, and the crucial elements in his army and his government were Turkish. Moreover, the success of war against the Europeans was intimately linked to the ambitions of these alien leaders who quarrelled amongst themselves and fought other Muslims as frequently as they engaged the western settlers. Saladin's empire was big, but its relatively weak structure, its many enemies, and its many obligations mean that size in itself was no guarantee of victory.

Hattin was a great triumph for Muslims, but it was only one victory in a war which would last until 1291. In 1187 Saladin defeated the Latin kingdom of Jerusalem and seized the Holy City of Jerusalem, but he was unable to destroy all the other western strongholds in the Holy Land. These were small, but this was a war which pitted him against the whole of European Latin Christendom whose defeat was beyond the reach of his military power. The result of Hattin was the launching of the Third Crusade which reconquered a substantial part of the old kingdom, and formed a permanent threat to the security of the Muslim states in the area. Thus in 1229 Jerusalem itself once more fell into western hands. This is why Saladin's triumph at Hattin was not truly decisive, and why, for a time at least, he was eclipsed by others in Muslim memory. The inconclusive nature of his victory has powerfully influenced the afterlife of Hattin. It is the purpose of this first chapter to explain how the violent hatred between Islam and western Christendom originated, how the crusade sprang from it, and how Islam reacted to this invasion. It is a story of hostility and intolerance. It is often pointed out that during the crusading period Europe and Islam traded and that there was much cultural interchange. This is certainly undeniable, but then much the same could be said of the West and the Soviet Union during their long confrontation between 1945 and 1989. Even so nobody could seriously doubt that the Cold War was marked by fear and contempt, death and destruction. And as in the Cold War, the collision of crusade and *jihad* was not simply ideological, but was entwined with baser motives of greed and personal ambition.

In the eleventh century three civilizations squatted around the Mediterranean. The richest and most extensive by far was Islam, reaching from Pakistan to Spain and from the Sudan to Tashkent deep in the great Eurasian steppe. The oldest was Byzantium, the eastern remnant of the Roman empire ruled from Constantinople, controlling Greece, much of southern Italy, most of the Balkans, and the western parts of Anatolia, with influence radiating out into Russia whose rulers had been converted by Byzantine missionaries. The weakest, poorest, and most divided was western Europe, which had only come into existence after the collapse of the western part of the Roman empire in the fifth century. There was no equilibrium, no balance, between these cultures, because all of them were torn by internal rivalries and subjected to violent change which spilled over the rather vague frontiers between them.

Islam became a major force in the world when, inspired by the teachings of Muhammad, the Arabs erupted out of Arabia into the Middle East in the seventh century. Muhammad died in 632, but by 635 his followers had driven the Byzantines out of Syria and Palestine and had seized their prized province of Egypt. Shortly thereafter, despite severe Byzantine resistance, North Africa too fell to them. East Rome was now confined to Asia Minor and parts of the Balkans, eastern Europe, and Italy. Between 633 and 651 Islam destroyed the old Persian empire and by 664 was making inroads into India. The warriors of Islam were inspired by the doctrine of *jihad*, the idea that war to conquer the world outside Islam, the *Dar al-Harb*, was a sacred duty. In 711 this ideological drive resulted in the conquest of almost all of Spain except for the small Christian realms of the north-west; this brought Islam into violent confrontation with western Europe. In 732 an army from Muslim Spain was defeated near Poitiers by the Carolingian warlord Charles Martel. He and his family had established a precarious domination over the Franks, the most powerful people in the former western part of the Roman empire, but had he been defeated, it is likely that the Muslims of Spain would have extended their power into Gaul. As it was, Muslim outposts in southern France continued to exist down to 973. Islamic rulers seized the Balearic islands, Corsica, and Sardinia. In 831 they began to conquer Byzantine Sicily, using it as a base to establish colonies in southern Italy. The onslaught on southern Italy by the Aghlabid emirs of Sicily seems to have had something of the character of a *jihad*, although here as elsewhere motives were mixed because these powerful rulers were trying to extend their authority. Muslim raiders established themselves in mainland Italy and in 847 burned St Peter's in Rome. As a result Pope Leo IV (847–55) built the Leonine wall to defend the Vatican. But the Muslims established bases on the River Garigliano only 100 kilometres from Rome and Pope John VIII (872–82) was forced to pay them tribute. Not until 915 were the Muslims driven from the Garigiliano, and even after that they maintained footholds in the area until the thirteenth century.

Across the western Mediterranean Muslim freebooters and pirates were at work. Until 973 their base near St Tropez enabled them to raid deep into the hinterland of southern France. At the end of the tenth century the armies of Muslim Spain drove into the petty Christian kingdoms in the north of the peninsula. In 997 they sacked the shrine of St James of Compostela, and followed this up with widespread devastation and raids into southern

France. It was only in 1017 that the kings of León recovered their capital. Ports such as Pisa and Genoa struggled to survive Muslim raids.[3] For 300 years Islamic states and adventurers harassed southern Europe under the flag of holy war, and these assaults embedded in western consciousness a real fear of Islam as an alien, aggressive, and deeply threatening religion, some sort of menacing paganism or monstrous perversion of Christianity whose success challenged the one true faith. One of the greatest European intellectuals of the Dark Ages, Bede, who lived in northern England far from the Islamic threat, nonetheless condemned these 'sons of Ishmael, whose hand is against every man' as adherents of false heresy, and rejoiced in their defeat by Charles Martel at the Battle of Poitiers in 732.[4]

At its height, between about 750 and 850, the empire of Islam was ruled by the caliphs of the Abbasid family, the 'Commanders of the Faithful' and successors of Muhammad, who united all sacred and secular authority and maintained a glorious court at Baghdad. Their world empire extended from southern France to the Sudan and from the Atlantic coast of Morocco to North India. In 751 the Arab governor of Tashkent defeated a Chinese army at the Battle of Atlakh on the Tal River, halting Chinese expansion into western Asia. Basra, in southern Iraq, traded vigorously with India, the Indonesian archipelago, and Guangzhou in southern China, spreading its new religion into the Far East. This gigantic empire never bent all its energies to the conquest of Europe because that area was much too poor to divert attention from richer parts of the world which were less remote from Islam's centres of power. However, local rulers in Spain, Sicily, and North Africa were strong enough to terrorize the coasts of southern Europe and threaten their rulers.

In the tenth century the huge Islamic empire fragmented. It had always been too big to be ruled directly, so in its outlying areas individual governors from the start enjoyed a high degree of independence. Such was the wealth and patronage of the caliph that the immense central court at Baghdad was torn by competing groups seeking power and advancement. The ultimate sanction of the caliphs was the possession of a strong army which could repel outside enemies and overawe subordinates, but this was very expensive to maintain. Moreover, the leaders of the army intrigued with the court factions to increase their wealth and influence. The caliphate was hereditary in the Abbasid family, but when, on the death of a caliph, there was no obvious adult male to succeed, civil wars erupted in Baghdad, and these increased in bitterness as competition for resources became sharper, enabling provincial governors to break away from the rule of the caliph. By 1050 the Abbasid caliphs were no more than figureheads, dominated by powerful courtiers, and their rule barely extended beyond the immediate surroundings of Baghdad. At the same time the luxury and constant quarrels of the court at Baghdad increased religious criticism. For Islam was not a monolithic religion and there was a long tradition of dissent whose focus was the succession to the caliphate.

The Abbasid family claimed descent from the Prophet, and they had always enjoyed the support of mainstream Sunni Muslims. However, there had always been dissenters, the Shi'ites, who believed that the caliphate should be vested in descendants of Ali, the son-in-law of Muhammad, who had been assassinated in 661. There were many Shi'ite groups, and amongst them there was no consensus on who should be the ruling caliph. They were scattered across the whole Muslim world, but they tended to be most important in marginal areas away from the centres of power where each developed their own ideas about the true descent from the Prophet and about Muslim law and faith. However, they all denounced the corruption of Baghdad and its 'false' caliphs and gained great credit from their co-religionists for doing so. North Africa (Maghrib) was a very long way from Baghdad and there a Shi'ite group arose whose leading family claimed descent from Fatima, the daughter of the Prophet. This line of Fatimid caliphs became established in Tunisia, but in 969 they conquered Cairo and quickly pushed into Palestine and Syria, claiming to be the true and universal heirs of the Prophet. Thus religious and political fragmentation tore apart the very heart of Islam. Far to the west, Muslim Spain (al-Andalus) broke up shortly after 1000, while turbulence in the North African states weakened Muslim hold on Sicily and the islands of the western Mediterranean.

At the time it seemed as if Byzantium would be the state which gained more than any other from the decline of the caliphate. Its armies went on the offensive, and in 969, the very year that the Fatimid caliphate was established in Cairo, the Byzantines seized Antioch which they had not held since 735. Subsequently they pushed their influence deep into Syria where Aleppo became a vassal state. But the Byzantine resurgence was halted in its tracks by the arrival in the Islamic heartlands of a new people, the Turks, who the caliphs employed as Mamluks, slave-soldiers. As Islam pushed out onto the steppe, its soldiers encountered these hardy and disciplined horse-archers. They were exceptional horsemen who lived almost all their lives in the saddle on the bleak steppe of southern Asia. Their weapon was the composite bow. It consisted of a wooden core, with bone glued to the inside and sinew to the outside. This made it formidably powerful despite being short enough to wield in the saddle. Horse archers had always existed in the Middle East, but their need to halt, or at least slow down, to fire had made them very vulnerable. As a result they had become only one element of a cavalry force in which lancers, either heavily or lightly armoured, predominated. By contrast, Turks could fire at the gallop and their way of life accustomed them to working together. Consequently they could approach their enemies in squadrons, moving quickly and firing volley after volley of arrows which were effective from about 80 metres, then turn away to try to outflank or even to surround the enemy. Al-Jahiz, a Muslim writer of the ninth century, commented on the speed of the Turks and the accuracy and rapidity of their fire:

> The Turk can shoot at beasts, birds, hoops, men, sitting quarry, dummies and birds on the wing, and do so at full gallop to fore or rear, to left or to right, upwards downwards, loosing ten arrows before the Kharijite [Arab tribesmen] can nock [put an arrow to the string] one.[5]

These horse archers would charge home only when hostile formations began to break up under their missile attack. Because each warrior had a string of horses, Turks could travel long distances quickly, or sustain very rapid movement on the battlefield. Turks first entered the Islamic world in the ninth century when they were employed by the caliphs as the cutting edge of their armies, and thereafter almost every potentate in the Islamic world sought to take some of them into service, even though such mercenary troops were very expensive. At the same time the Turks of the steppe, through long contact with the settled Middle East, converted to Islam, and their leaders began to create states.

The Seljuq family united sizeable numbers of tribes and moved into Khurasan in eastern Iran. Their most important leader, Tughrul Bey, quickly recognized the weakness at the heart of Islam. In 1055, in conjunction with the Turkish soldiers who were already there, he occupied Baghdad, and assumed the title of sultan, creating a Seljuq empire centred on Iran and Iraq. From this time onwards, right down to 1919, the Middle Eastern heartlands of Islam would generally be ruled by Turks. The sultans were Sunni and therefore respected the religious authority of the caliphs, but cut them off from influence on political matters. As champions of the true religion, the Seljuqs were able to justify their war against the Fatimids of Egypt, whom they drove from Jerusalem in 1073.

Many Turkish tribes did not wish to be incorporated into the Seljuq empire, and some of them, while acknowledging the nominal overlordship of the sultan, tried to carve out principalities of their own in Byzantine Anatolia. Because they were fighting Christians their ambitions could be represented as holy war, and this helped to draw Turks from the steppe eager for a share of loot and land. Their raids were highly destructive and, because they were 'hit-and-run', very difficult to counter. The emperor Romanus IV (1068–71) adopted a strategy of attacking Seljuq Syria in order to force the sultan to curb their raids. In 1071 Romanus IV led a major expedition towards Syria, in an attempt to force the sultan to stop the attackers. Because they were nominally his vassals, the sultan could not stand by and watch the tribes being crushed by a Christian enemy because this would have undermined his prestige as a champion of Islam. Therefore, in alliance with them he defeated and captured Romanus at the Battle of Manzikert. This defeat should not have been as significant as it was. The sultan had no wish to see the dissident tribes expand into Byzantine territory, and in any case was anxious to renew his war against the Fatimids. For these reasons he quickly freed Romanus IV and imposed only moderate terms of peace on his empire including a payment of tribute. But Romanus had many enemies amongst the Byzantine aristocracy who denounced the peace as shameful and combined to overthrow him. They then turned on one another in a bitter civil war over rule of the empire during which the Turkish tribes made inroads into Anatolia. Even worse, Byzantine factions bought their military support in return for handing over the cities and provinces of Anatolia. By the time the emperor Alexius Comnenus (1081–1118) restored stability, the lands of Byzantium were largely confined to Europe. Turkish princes dominated much of the Aegean coast of Anatolia, almost to within sight of Constantinople, and Nicaea, the city where the Christian Creed had been formulated in 325, was the capital of a new sultan of Rhum (Romania, the land of the Romans).

At the same time western Europe was growing in wealth and confidence. Its feeble states, although mutually hostile, recognized a certain common culture. At its heart was the Church which used Latin as a common language, and was headed by the bishop of Rome whose authority, while ill-defined, was universally accepted as final in matters spiritual. Government was in the hands of a narrow aristocracy who drew their riches almost entirely from land, and from these were selected kings whose power over their nobility was fairly limited. This was because kings did not have sufficient resources to support complex and organized administrations, and therefore they depended everywhere upon their landed lords for local government. All over Europe the members of the leading noble families looked back to the time of the Frankish king Charlemagne (768–814) as a golden age because he had for a time united all Europe. They claimed descent from his family and its most important noble followers. Legends were woven about these distant ancestors which became an important part of aristocratic culture. Charlemagne, it was believed, had saved Constantinople, seat of the Roman empire of the East, from Islamic attack. One of his paladins was commemorated in the great epic poem, the *Song of Roland*, as a hero who fell in battle against the Muslims of Spain. By the early eleventh century western Europe was conscious of its own identity and was expanding. German powers were attempting to subjugate the pagan peoples of northern and central Europe and to convert them to Catholic Christianity. In Spain the tiny Christian kingdoms of the north began to make inroads into al-Andalus, the Muslim south of the peninsula. In Italy the Islamic settlements on the mainland were destroyed or subjugated. Norman settlers in southern Italy, who probably first came to the area as pilgrims en route to Jerusalem, expelled Byzantium from the area by 1071, and thereafter proceeded to conquer Muslim Sicily. The trading cities of the Italian littoral began to threaten the Islamic hold on the islands of the western Mediterranean and to push their trade eastwards.

In the period after the collapse of Charlemagne's empire, Europe had been attacked by many external enemies. The Magyars, a Turkish people settled in Hungary, raided the West and were only crushed in 955 at the Battle of the Lech, after which they were gradually converted to Catholic Christianity. The Scandinavians, whom we remember as the Vikings, were still sometimes dangerous in the early eleventh century. Yet, generally speaking, by about 1000 the stabilization of political authorities in Europe and the process of Christianization of surrounding peoples had first reduced the sense of threat and then led to an aggressive expansionism at the expense of their neighbours. The great exception to this was Islam. Although Europeans were enjoying some successes in Spain and elsewhere, the sense of a looming and enormous power, capable of resurgence at any moment, remained. And in the centuries of threat the idea had grown that to slay those who did not believe in Christ was not the same as killing fellow Christians and more acceptable to God— that it was, in some senses, holy war. It has to be stressed that no doctrine, or even authoritative statement, underpinned this notion which remained totally undefined. Nonetheless it was frequently and at times almost casually articulated.

This was possible because Christianity had no doctrine of war. In contrast, in Islam the notion of *jihad* was rooted in the Koran and carefully developed by legalists, often in remarkably humanitarian ways. Christianity simply clung to its belief that slaying a human being in whatever circumstances was an appalling sin, demanding a heavy penance if the killer were not to suffer the torments of hell. This idea, however, existed alongside more pragmatic behaviour. Violence was essential to the maintenance of peace and order within Christian society and for its defence from external enemies. As St Augustine remarked:

> Surely it is not without purpose that we have the institution of the power of kings, the death penalty of the judge, the barbed hooks of the executioner, the weapons of the soldier, the right of punishment of the overlord, even the severity of the good father. All those things have their methods, their causes, their reasons, their practical benefits.[6]

Such thinking eroded the principle that all taking of human life was murder and equally wicked. As a result, in time killing in war for the public good came to carry a lighter penance than causing death for private reasons such as gain or revenge. Thus an eighth-century book of penance ascribed to the Reverend Bede demands:

> He who slays a layman with malice aforethought or for the possession of his inheritance, four years [of penance].
> He who slays in public war, forty days.[7]

'Public war', of course, covered a multitude of situations, because laymen fought for a wide variety of reasons, and so did warrior-bishops, some of whom were even sanctified despite, or perhaps because of, this behaviour. Nevertheless men and women of the upper class were deeply aware of the fundamental contradiction between the prohibition on killing and the practicalities of their way of life. Individuals reconciled this contradiction by penance, performing good deeds or acts of self-deprivation which would ameliorate their sufferings in the afterlife. In 1066 the Norman army in England, concerned about the souls of its men who had killed so many Anglo-Saxons, accepted a penance which assumed that each man had killed three enemies. If it had been performed personally such a penalty would have demobilized the Norman army for at least two years, so gifts were made to monks who would then say the necessary prayers and appropriate fasts. Wealthy laymen often gave to churches or founded new ones in what amounted to fire insurance—insurance against the fires of hell.

Another form of penance was pilgrimage to the shrine of a saint, because any journey was dangerous and removed the penitent from the circle of family and friends. And of all such journeys, that to Jerusalem commanded a special place in the minds of European people. It was not only the most distant and therefore most expensive and dangerous of all pilgrimages, but its destination was the most sacred of all Christian sites. Such a pilgrimage, it was thought, deserved remission of penance for all the sins that a person might have committed. Fulk Nerra, count of Anjou (987–1039), established one of the most powerful principalities in France by ruthless violence. Yet he founded the great abbey of Beaulieu and travelled at least three times to Jerusalem, dying at Metz on the return from his final visit. And lesser men too were deeply concerned with the good of their souls. In and about the year 1000, the millennium of the birth of Christ, huge numbers of pilgrims went to Jerusalem, while in 1033, the millennium of His Passion, a contemporary recorded:

> At this time an innumerable multitude of people from the whole world, greater than any man before could have hoped to see, began to travel to the Sepulchre of the Saviour at Jerusalem. First to go were the petty people, then those of middling estate, and next the powerful, kings, counts, marquesses and bishops; finally, and this was something that had never happened before, numerous women, noble and poor, undertook the journey.[8]

In 1064 a vast crowd accompanied some leading German bishops to Jerusalem, but their ostentatious display of riches resulted in an attack by brigands:

> In the meantime the bishops travelling to Jerusalem unwisely revealed their great wealth to the people through whose lands they were passing, though divine mercy should have restrained them from this folly. The barbarians came in great numbers from the fields and the cities to see these famous men. At first the rich and well-equipped pilgrims thought this was a miracle, but they had come only in hope of plunder...they entered the lands of the Saracens and came to a town called Ramla. They departed from the houses there and at about

the third hour on the day before Easter they were attacked by Arabs who, seeing the arrival of such obviously wealthy men, had come together armed in large numbers hoping to seize wealth.[9]

As Europe expanded in the eleventh century the notion grew that war against 'outsiders' was different, more righteous, perhaps even meritorious, and this was particularly welcome as it added a moral justification for the seizure of pagan lands. Closely connected to this was the sense of Islam as a particularly dangerous enemy. European aristocratic culture was deeply infused by hatred of Islam, provoked by centuries of Muslim attack which had been especially intense in Italy where the papacy formed the very religious and cultural heart of the emerging West.

At the same time the papacy was grappling on its own account with the idea that violence could have worthwhile and positive ends. The wars against Islam in Spain and Italy were extending the Church and the popes wanted to control this process. More urgently, after 1073 the papacy became embroiled with the German emperor whose control of Italy threatened its independence. In this long war, usually called the Investiture Contest, the popes claimed to be the supreme authority in Christendom to counter the pretensions of the emperor to dominate Rome and the Church. To defend themselves they needed military assistance. This was by no means entirely novel. As Italian princes the popes had often recruited their own troops and enlisted allies. But they were now waging war to bolster their spiritual position, and their enemies demanded to know how the representative of the 'Prince of Peace' could do that. This was a war of ideas, about who should be the supreme authority in Christendom, and it was being fought in the new and more intensely religious atmosphere of the eleventh century. It was essential, therefore, albeit rather difficult, to justify the shedding of blood in the name of Christ. In this new situation there emerged papal propagandists, the 'theologians of violence' like Anselm of Lucca who tried to justify papal actions, but their work was not well known and sacred violence remained problematic.

Pope Urban II (1088–99) effectively ended this gap between theology and practice. He wanted to help the Christians of Spain to recover land from the Muslims, and in 1089 he wrote to some of the Spanish lords offering the full remission of sin normally attached to the Jerusalem pilgrimage to any who would fight the Muslims and help in the reconstruction of the ancient and strategically placed city of Tarragona:

> We beg all who may be going to Jerusalem or other places in penance and devotion that they should expend all that they have saved for their journey on the restoration of the city of Tarragona, so that with God's aid it may have a bishop and cathedral and its people may be protected from the Saracens by a wall and forewall. To such people we promise all that was offered to them for going to more distant places.[10]

This linkage between the Jerusalem indulgence and fighting against the Muslims played a very important part in Urban's thinking in 1095 when he launched what we call the First Crusade. In this letter to Tarragona Urban was offering what was later called an indulgence, the substitution of one kind of penance—in this case killing Muslims in order to liberate Tarragona—for other more traditional forms like self-denial, almsgiving, or building churches. Killing thus became a positive act equal to making a charitable donation, and effectively created a new path to heaven—salvation through slaughter.

In 1094 Urban II decided that he needed to reassert papal influence in Gaul where the Church, in his view, was in need of reform. On his way there in March 1095, he held a church council in north Italy at Piacenza where he encountered a delegation from the eastern emperor Alexius I (1081–1118). They asked the pope to use his influence to persuade western mercenaries to go to Constantinople and serve in the imperial army. The loss of Anatolia to the Turks had weakened the eastern empire because this was its traditional recruiting-ground. While the new Turkish principalities in Anatolia were not especially strong and had usually resisted the authority of Baghdad, they could always on religious grounds invoke the support of the sultan against any aggression from Byzantium. But in 1092 the great sultan Malik Shah (1072–92) died, and the Seljuq family was rent by a bitter and complex succession dispute. This isolated the feuding principalities of Anatolia and offered to Alexius an opportunity to recover at least some lost territory. But if he was to achieve anything he needed to mount a credible military threat to his enemies. He may have lacked the old recruiting grounds of Anatolia, but his empire remained immensely rich and he could afford to employ mercenaries. The fighting qualities of western knights were widely recognized in the Mediterranean lands, and they were often employed even by Muslim powers. Alexius already had many of them in his army. He seems to have hoped to increase their numbers substantially by exploiting friendship with the pope, whom he had been courting for some time. Pope Urban duly asked the assembled church dignitaries to try to persuade soldiers to help Alexius.

But the importance of Alexius' appeal was that it seems to have stimulated Urban's thinking. He passed into France, and after consulting with Raymond, count of Toulouse and Adhemar, bishop of Le Puy, both of whom were later to become leading participants in the First Crusade, convened a church council at Clermont on 18 November 1095. There, on 27 November, Urban appealed for a great expedition to aid the Christians of the East and to free Jerusalem from the domination of Islam, and he promised: 'If any man sets out from pure devotion, not for reputation or monetary gain, to liberate the church of God at Jerusalem, his journey shall be reckoned in place of all penance.'[11]

This was essentially the same idea—salvation through slaughter—that Urban had already invoked on behalf of Tarragona. But it was now set to serve a much greater aim, the liberation of Jerusalem which was so important to European Christians. And Urban elaborated the idea to insist upon the linkage between war and sanctity. He seems to have insisted that all who went on this journey should perform penance and take a public vow, and in token of this promise, they should wear the sign of the cross on their breast on the outward journey and on their back as they returned. This ritual by which people took the cross closely resembled that of the pilgrim. In addition, it was decreed that the lands of departed crusaders should be protected by the 'Peace of God'. Urban did not really provide a definition of Christian holy war, but his proclamation at Clermont offered an authoritative statement that as long as it was at the behest of the papacy, war was not merely permissible, but actually could earn favour in the sight of God. This was accompanied by a bitterly anti-Islamic rhetoric which portrayed the fellow Christians of the East suffering at the hands of

a people rejected by God, indeed *a generation that set not their heart aright, and whose spirit was not steadfast with God*, has invaded the land of those

Christians [of the East], depopulated them by slaughter and plunder and arson ... They throw down the altars after soiling them with their own filth, circumcise Christians, and pour the resulting blood either on the altars or into the baptismal vessels.[12]

Papal authority was enormously enhanced by the success of the appeal which generated a huge army some 60,000 strong.

Clearly Urban's appeal struck a nerve with the European upper classes for whom war was a way of life. They were a tiny minority of the population who controlled almost all the riches in their world. They justified this astonishing power by claiming that they protected society against external attack and internal rebellion. Contemporaries saw the elements of society as having been appointed by God and having reciprocal duties. In the words of Gerald, bishop of Cambrai (1012–51): 'from the beginning, mankind has been divided into three parts, among men of prayer, farmers, and men of war'.[13]

The upper class certainly used their wealth for military purposes. Proficiency in the practice of arms was time-consuming and demanded great resources which were created by taxes drawn from the population as a whole. But the upper class knew perfectly well that much of their violence was directed not to the protection of society but to the advancement of their own interests and rivalries. As an example, in 1089 two Norman lords, William of Breteuil and Ascelin Goel, embarked on a protracted war after a quarrel over a woman. In the course of the conflict William ravaged the countryside and extorted money from peasants, financing his army 'with the help of ransoms of captives and plunder taken from country people'.[14] Moreover, they knew that the values of their warrior ethic—ferocity, bravery, and loyalty to their lord—conflicted with those of the

Christian religion. The warrior, therefore, was at risk of eternal damnation, which is why so many so often made gifts to churches in search of prayers which might save their souls. But Urban flattered their bravery and praised their values, so long as their energies were directed to what he saw as a proper end, the liberation of Jerusalem. Moreover, although he was careful to lay down that spiritual reward was only available to those who went on the expedition 'out of pure devotion', he did not condemn their acquisition of 'reputation or monetary gain'. It was this powerful cocktail, this heady mix of opportunities for divine forgiveness and worldly glory, that energized the European aristocracy.

Moreover, in 1095 the military aristocracy of Europe did not know that the crusade would be a continuing phenomenon, but saw the appeal of Clermont as a sudden and momentary opening of a window of opportunity, truly a pathway to heaven. At the same time, Urban's rhetoric exploited the bitter hatred of Islam embodied in the culture of the upper class which had been bred by centuries of Muslim attacks.

This message of holy war was energetically propagated by Urban who toured southern France trying to persuade the nobles and knights of the area to join his expedition, and wrote letters to other parts of Europe soliciting support. The clergy who attended Clermont preached to the same end, but Urban's message was enormously amplified by those monks who served in the network of monasteries centred on the abbey of Cluny which was responsible to the Holy See. They and similar orders reached across Europe and they were devoted to the cause of the papacy. These monks were the spiritual advisers of many of the upper class, and their influence must have been decisive in bringing numerous important families over to the cause of the crusade. And every great noble family stood at the tip of a *mouvance*, a network of influence and relationships, so that when one member of the family took the cross, his followers were obliged, at the very least, to think seriously about doing so as well.

But what gave Urban's appeal permanence and prestige was its success, the astonishing fact that on 15 July 1099 the First Crusade captured Jerusalem and threw off the bonds of Islam which had for so long controlled the Holy Land. There were many reasons for this outcome, but ultimately it was rooted in the religious enthusiasm which culminated in a massacre around the holy sites of Islam on the Temple Mount at Jerusalem. This was an age which considered that the outcome of battle was God's will, so that the seizure of Jerusalem after a long and bitter campaign was seen as part of God's continuing plan for mankind. As a result, crusading received a lasting and prominent place in the western religious consciousness. In practical terms this created a profound sense of obligation to support and assist the Latin states of the Middle East founded by the success of the First Crusade.

The earliest of these was centred on the ancient city of Edessa (now called Urfa or Şanlıurfa in eastern Turkey). The Turkish conquest of Anatolia in the 1070s had not destroyed the existing populations of the area, and Edessa lay within a zone dominated by Christian Armenian settlement. In the confusion caused by the death of the Turkish sultan Malik Shah in 1092 the city became independent under an Armenian ruler: 'Theodore [Thoros]... was in Edessa, which he had saved from the Turks, expecting to hand it over to the emperor.'[15] By the time of the arrival of the First Crusade in Syria in 1097, Edessa was under heavy Turkish pressure, and the city begged the western army for help. This arrived in the person of one of its lesser leaders, Baldwin of Boulogne, brother of Godfrey de Bouillon who became the first ruler of Jerusalem in 1099. Baldwin soon overthrew Thoros and established the Latin principality of Edessa. Its fall to the Muslims, led by Zengi of Aleppo in 1144, provoked the calling of the Second Crusade (1145–9), a fiasco which achieved nothing. Antioch became a Latin principality when it was conquered by the First Crusade in June 1098, after which it was seized by the south Italian leader Bohemond. The Byzantines claimed that this city should have been handed over to them in consequence of the agreement reached between Alexius and the crusader leaders at Constantinople in spring 1097; by this the Greeks provided aid and alliance and the western leaders promised to return former imperial territory. As a result crusader Antioch was dogged by Byzantine hostility. The kingdom of Jerusalem was established immediately after the capture of the city, the very climax of the First Crusade, in July 1099, and entrusted to Godfrey de Bouillon whose dynasty would hold it right down to Hattin and beyond. It is distinguished by being the only one of these states to be a kingdom. The county of Tripoli arose from the ambitions of one of the leaders of the First Crusade, Raymond, count of Toulouse, though he died in 1105 and it was only in 1109 that the city of Tripoli finally fell to his son Bertrand.

The existence of these outposts of western Catholicism in the Holy Land created a continuing obligation upon western men and women, for everybody knew that they were small and threatened islands in the sea of Islam. And the Church took every opportunity to remind people of the need to succour the Holy Land, not least by the great annual feast for the liberation of Jerusalem which commemorated the crusader capture of the city. This momentous event was seen as a revelation of God's will. One of the original crusaders, Raymond of Aguilers, wrote an account of the crusade in which he asserted that the liberation of Jerusalem on the Feast of the Dispersion of the Apostles was no less than a reclaiming of the Holy Places, a closing of the circle opened as the Apostles set out on their missionary vocation. Potted accounts of the capture of the Holy City designed to be read at this feast are contained in European manuscripts. Crusading, it is often forgotten, was a religious exercise, a path to salvation. Even their Muslim enemies came to realize that this was what drove them on. At the time of the Third Crusade, which was an attempt to recapture the kingdom of Jerusalem after the Battle of Hattin, Ibn al-Athir noted the following story:

> A certain Frankish captive told me that he was his mother's only son. They possessed no worldly goods other than a house which she sold and used the purchase money to equip him and send him to free [Jerusalem] and that he was taken prisoner. This is an extreme example of the religious and spiritual motivation that the Franks had. They came forth on every variety of mount, by land and by sea, from every nook and cranny. Had God not shown his grace to the Muslims.... people would be saying, 'Syria and Egypt used to belong to the Muslims.' This explains why they left their homes.[16]

Of course only a minority of western Europeans ever availed themselves of this path to salvation, but its legitimacy was fixed in the minds of virtually all western Catholics. After the First Crusade there were many families with a crusading tradition, and this was extended to others by marriage. The contagion of crusading, therefore, spread across the European upper class, creating new loyalties and connections. The astonishing success of 1099 fixed the Holy Places deep in the hearts of Europeans and firmly attached the need to defend them into their obligations as the military defenders of Christendom. Many, of course, never tried to act upon this, but none could deny it and so, in particular circumstances, a fanatical spirit could be aroused.

Spiritual concern was reinforced by material interests. The great aristocrats of the settler states almost all came from obscure origins, providing an example to younger sons seeking to make their way. Guy and Amalric, younger brothers of the important Poitevin family of Lusignan, went to the Latin kingdom in the 1170s and both rose to be kings of Jerusalem and Cyprus. Gerard of Ridefort came to the East as a mercenary hoping for a lordship; when he was disappointed in this he joined the Templar order and later became its grand master and a major force in the politics of Jerusalem. Of course these were all exceptional cases, but they set a powerful example, and it should always be remembered that people travel in hope, even though that may ultimately be frustrated. Humbler persons also found their way to the East. There was no land bridge to Jerusalem because Anatolia remained largely in Turkish hands, but even so there was substantial immigration into the kingdom of Jerusalem from Europe. Peasants, petty artisans, and traders established themselves, many of them thriving on the needs of pilgrims who arrived in Jerusalem in the summer months. They came by sea, and this introduces one of the most remarkable phenomena of the crusading age.

The First Crusade had enjoyed important support from Genoa and Pisa. As a consequence these relatively small trading cities were able to establish trading bases in the cities of the Palestinian littoral and to tap into the trade in the luxury goods of the Far East, especially spices. They were quickly joined by the long-established and great trading port of Venice whose fleet played a major role in the capture of Tyre in 1124. The shipping of these city states brought pilgrims and settlers to the Holy Land. The effect of this was to establish a western naval supremacy in the eastern Mediterranean which rapidly eclipsed and forced into decline the naval power of Egypt. These maritime links with the West were vitally important to the crusader states. In 1102 Baldwin I of Jerusalem (1100–18) was defeated by the Egyptians and fled, accompanied by a very small remnant of his army, but they were sufficiently reinforced by the arrival of a ships carrying pilgrims to fight off their enemies. When Baldwin III (1143–63) besieged Ascalon in 1153 arriving pilgrims were drafted willy-nilly into the royal army. It is difficult to see how the settler states could have survived without the Italian city states, whose prosperity in turn grew on eastern trade. By the thirteenth century they were even transporting Muslim trade along the North African coast. We should not, however, assume that the Italians simply wanted wealth: they too were Catholics, susceptible to the appeal of religion. Indeed, Muslim ports like Alexandria had always welcomed them, but Italian traders seem to have preferred to work in an environment dominated by their fellow Catholics. The West, therefore, was bound to the new settler states of the Latin East by a complex web of personal, family, religious, and commercial links.

Religious belief was central to crusading, and nothing reveals this more clearly than the rise of the military orders and the astonishing volume of imitation which they inspired. To the modern mind the idea of fighting monks is deeply alien, yet that is what the Templars were—men sworn to the vocation of war against the infidel who were also subject to the monastic vows of poverty, chastity, and obedience. The Temple originated in a group of nine pious knights led by Hugues de Payens who seem to have taken upon themselves the task of protecting pilgrims on the dangerous roads from the coast to Jerusalem. It was not unusual for knights to come to the Holy Land for a short period, but this group had apparently determined to stay, and took monastic vows, and in the year 1118 approached King Baldwin II for accommodation in the Holy City. He allocated to them quarters in the former al-Aqsa mosque on the Temple Mount which then served as the royal palace. It was built on the supposed site of Solomon's Temple, hence the name Templar. At the Council of Troyes in 1129 the order was officially endorsed by the Church and promptly began to receive enormous donations from the faithful all over the West.

The Hospital was originally founded in the early eleventh century by merchants of Amalfi as a house to care for pilgrims in the city of Jerusalem. At that time a hospital might care for the sick, but its main function was to provide hospitality for pious travellers, and it was, therefore, in no way military. Its master at the time of the First Crusade was Gerard who was imprisoned during the crusader siege of 1099. The story is told that the garrison commander forced him to stand on the walls to throw stones at the crusaders, but that he threw bread rolls instead. However that may be, the order became very famous, establishing hospitals along the pilgrim routes to the Holy City and developing notable medicinal knowledge. By 1136 it was certainly using its immense wealth for military purposes because in that year it took over the castle of Beth Gibelin. The two orders soon enjoyed papal immunity, by which their masters were responsible not to the king of Jerusalem, but to the pope, which meant that effectively they were independent. Astonishingly, King Alfonso I of Aragon (1104–34), facing death without an heir, drew up a will dividing his kingdom between the Templars and the Hospitallers, along with a third organization, the knightly confraternity of the Holy Sepulchre. The will was never implemented, but that it was ever made is an indication of the high esteem in which the fighting monks were held. And in consequence the two orders received vast lands in Aragon. And this generosity was replicated all over Europe. There is evidence all about us of the extraordinary esteem in which they were held. In England, for example, there are many Templars' Woods, while Bristol Temple Meads is the main station in that city. The Templars built round churches, facsimiles of the Holy Sepulchre at Jerusalem; obvious examples of these are the Temple in London, which now serves as the centre of the legal profession, and the Round Church of Holy Sepulchre in Cambridge, but they are found all across Europe.

The orders of the Temple and the Hospital had enormous prestige. They were deeply respected as the sworn defenders of Jerusalem. But they were also monks whose prayers, it was believed, could help to relieve the burden of sin of ordinary sinful people. Individual members were admired because they had taken up the harsh life of a soldier, yet like all monks, they sacrificed personal liberty and all self-indulgence, but these were the traditional pleasures and compensations of the warrior life. Thus the orders had a double appeal, particularly to the kings and aristocrats of Europe, and this was why they received such enormous gifts from the laity.

The scale of these holdings enabled the orders to create powerful armies and to sustain mighty castles in the Latin states. By the

1170s the Temple and the Hospital in the kingdom of Jerusalem seem each to have been able to raise 300 knights who were supported by turcopoles (light cavalry) and foot soldiers and supplemented in times of need by mercenaries. In effect they formed standing armies, the backbone of the fighting forces of the western settlers. This was extraordinary because in the Middle Ages standing regular forces barely existed. Kings might keep a nucleus of soldiers about them, but major armies were gathered only for short periods, and then dispersed, because they cost so much and were, therefore, such a burden upon the king. In the 1190s Richard the Lionheart (1189–99) proposed to raise a standing army of some 300 knights. To support such a force for a year would have cost about half his ordinary annual income of £20,000 from England. In 1214 an alliance of England, Germany, and Flanders launched two great expeditions against the French king. In total each side seems to have raised about 2,000 knights, but they were only in the field for a few months. In the context of twelfth-century Europe each of the orders was a major military power, and this great strength was derived from the esteem in which they were held and the importance of Jerusalem to western people.

In fact the Temple and the Hospital were so widely admired that they were widely imitated, especially in Spain where knightly fraternities sworn to fight the Muslims appear as early as the 1120s. These gave birth to such famous institutions as the orders of Santiago and Calatrava (1164) and the great Order of Alcantara (1177). The Teutonic Order was established by Germans at Acre in 1190 during the Third Crusade as both a caring and a fighting order on the Hospitaller model, and it went on to become a very important element in the defence of the Holy Land. After 1291 it transferred most of its activities to the Baltic and became vitally important in the expansion of Catholic Christendom in northern Europe. The history of the orders, and their multiplication, is clear evidence of the religious devotion of European peoples and the way in which it was enlisted in the service of the crusade.

# 2

# Crusade and *Jihad*

When the First Crusade came, the fractured state of Islam made any united response impossible. The Fatimids of Egypt saw the crusaders as allies against their Turkish Sunni enemies and actually made an agreement with them. In February 1098 a delegation from Egypt arrived at Antioch and, according to Stephen of Blois, one of the crusader leaders: 'The Emperor of Babylon sent his Saracen envoys with letters to us in camp, and by this means he established peace and concord with us.'[1] When the crusaders went on to attack Jerusalem it was too late for the Fatimids to find allies. For some twenty years they were the most consistent enemies of the Latin kingdom of Jerusalem, but as Shi'ites they were reluctant to ally with the Sunni Turks of the north.

It was the convulsions within the Seljuq empire which opened the gates of Syria to the First Crusade. On Malik Shah's death his brother, Tutush Shah, who had been his regent in Syria, was at first well placed to gain the throne, but on 26 February 1095 (16 Safar, 488) Tutush was defeated and killed by Malik Shah's son, Barkyaruq, at the Battle of Dashlu. This did not end the conflict because others put forward claims to be sultan. Further west the sons of Tutush—Ridwan of Aleppo and Duqaq of

Damascus—were bitter rivals for their father's inheritance in Syria. The fighting between them meant that their subordinate governors, like Yaghi Siyan of Antioch who owed allegiance to Ridwan, could exploit the situation to acquire a high degree of independence. These rivalries in the Seljuq family triggered anxieties and tensions within the Muslim powers so that at the very moment of the arrival of the First Crusade, in October 1097, Ridwan's chief of police in Aleppo tried to mount a coup against him.[2]

Many Muslims seem to have regarded the crusade as simply another Byzantine army which would go away—as they so often had in the past. Moreover, *jihad* could only be proclaimed against a non-Muslim enemy, but there had really been no such threat for the last few centuries during which all wars pitted Muslim against Muslim. In spring 1098 the sultan had proclaimed *jihad* in support of Kerbogah's expedition to raise the crusader siege of Antioch and it had attracted many religious volunteers (*ghazi*). But the sultan was soon enmeshed in problems in Iran and Iraq. Al-Sulami, a Damascene jurist, was exceptional in understanding clearly the nature of the attack and in 1105 in his *Kitab al-Jihad* called for a *jihad* against the westerners.[3] But Ridwan and Duqaq were primarily concerned with local matters. The governors of cities like Shaizar, Homs, and the cities of the coast had allowed the First Crusade free passage, though Jewish Haifa was hostile, probably because they were aware that some crusaders had massacred the Jews of the Rhineland, regarding them as 'enemies within'. The chronicles of Aleppo and Damascus are concerned with local matters and treat only briefly the capture of Jerusalem by the First Crusade in 1099. Possibly this reflects the fact that the city had been seized by the Fatimids in July 1098, taking advantage of the Turks' preoccupation with the crusade and its attack on Antioch.

In time the Islamic powers recognized that the Europeans were establishing a threatening permanency. At the same time the western settlers lost the ideological unity of the First Crusade, and became preoccupied by their own interests. The northern states of Edessa and Antioch together posed a dangerous threat to Aleppo. By contrast the kingdom of Jerusalem saw opportunities for expansion towards Damascus and Egypt. The county of Tripoli, the smallest and last of the Latin states to be founded (1109), tended to play off the northern states against Jerusalem in order to maintain a degree of independence. These significant differences of alignment were masked for a time because the first two rulers of Jerusalem, Baldwin I (1100–18) and Baldwin II (1118–31), were exceptionally able men who had both ruled Edessa and took considerable interest in the north. But Edessa and Antioch were never strong enough or sufficiently close in their alliance to seize Aleppo. In 1126 rule of Aleppo fell to a powerful and able Muslim lord, Zengi of Mosul, who gradually pushed them onto the defensive. After the accession of Fulk I of Jerusalem (1131–43) the divergence between the northern states and Jerusalem became very evident, while the rulers of Antioch and Edessa were jealous of one another. It was in these circumstances that Zengi was able to seize Edessa in 1144, a success for Islam which provoked the Second Crusade. The rise of Muslim power under Zengi's son, Nur ad-Din, in the 1150s and 1160s somewhat curbed the separatism of Antioch and Tripoli, though they never coordinated their foreign policies with Jerusalem.

The concern of the European settlers for their own territorial and dynastic affairs was very evident. The military orders, in theory devoted to defending the Holy Land, behaved in much the same way. Both orders were formally subject only to the authority of the pope, but in their early years this had hardly mattered because they cooperated with the kings of Jerusalem and the other princes. But the immense riches given to them in Europe made them arrogant so that by the middle of the twelfth century they cooperated with the king of Jerusalem and the other princes only when it suited them. As the pressures of war impoverished many of the great lords of the East, the orders exploited their vast wealth in Europe, which was immune from enemy attack, to purchase vast territories and numerous castles in the Latin states. In 1142 Count Raymond II of Tripoli sold much of the east of his county—including the fortress of Crac des Chevaliers—to the Hospital which thereafter conducted their own policy towards the Muslims, quite independently of the count. The Temple and the Hospital became so quarrelsome and absorbed in their own territorial interests that they were censored by the pope in 1179. In 1168 the Temple refused to join King Amalric I (1163–74) in his attack on Egypt. In 1173 Amalric received a delegation from a Muslim sect, the Assassins, who held a strategically important enclave adjacent to Christian lands in the Nosairi mountains of Syria. The Assassins felt threatened by the growing power of Nur ad-Din, and so they proposed a treaty of friendship with the Europeans. King Amalric readily agreed, but this would have ended the annual tribute of 2,000 *besants* which the Assassins were paying to the Templars who held nearby fortresses. The Templar response was to murder the Assassin envoy as he returned, thus torpedoing the agreement. When the king demanded that the killers be handed over, the grand master resisted on the grounds that the order was subject to the pope alone. Amalric was enraged, and it was only his death in 1174 that prevented a major split between the kingdom and the order.

Effectively, by the 1170s the Temple and the Hospital had become independent forces within the Latin states.

An exactly opposite process, of consolidation, was taking place in Muslim Syria. In the wake of the First Crusade, with Catholic Christendom having gained a foothold as far east as the Euphrates, the possibilities for future expansion seemed endless. But they were not. The capture of Jerusalem in 1099 provoked an enormous wave of popular enthusiasm in Europe, as a result of which a new expedition, the 'Crusade of 1101', was launched. But it lacked unity and its commanders were not particularly able and as a result it was destroyed by a coalition of the Muslim powers of Syria and Anatolia. In 1102 Baldwin I of Jerusalem was defeated at Ramla by the Egyptian Fatimids and in 1104 the allied armies of Antioch and Edessa were crushed at Harran. All this encouraged their Islamic enemies. The sultans of Baghdad were deeply preoccupied by conflicts in Persia and the East, but they could not be seen to be indifferent to the extension of Christian power, so occasionally they lent their authority to wars against the western intruders.

The focus of the conflict between Catholic and Muslim was at first Aleppo whose ruler, Ridwan (1094–1113), feared Christian Antioch and yet was reluctant to seek help from Damascus or Baghdad lest it undermine his independence. In addition, within Aleppo there was a sharp division between Sunni and Shi'ites which weakened his regime. In fact Ridwan encouraged the new sect of the Assassins to establish themselves in the city because they were highly disciplined, and their espousal of political killing as an instrument of policy cowed his enemies. In 1110 or 1111 the citizens of Aleppo appealed for help over Ridwan's head to the sultan, who responded by gathering a large army under the command of Mawdoud, lord of Mosul and Sokman. But Ridwan feared them as much as he feared the Franks, and his refusal to help led to the break-up of their army. Ridwan's death in 1113 precipitated an even more serious crisis in the affairs of Aleppo. His son and successor, Alp Arslan, was persuaded by the sultan to massacre the Assassins of Aleppo, but this merely removed one of the pillars of Ridwan's government. In fact Alp Arslan turned out to be a perverse tyrant who was murdered, leaving power in the hands of a coterie of eunuchs who ruled in the name of another of Ridwan's sons, and appealed for help to the sultan. When the sultan responded by sending a large army under Bursuq, Tughtegin of Damascus allied with Aleppo against them and together they joined forces with Roger, prince of Antioch. Roger was a Christian, but he was first and foremost ruler of Antioch, so he was perfectly prepared to ally with Muslim powers. However, 'The Atabeg[4] [Tughtegin] forbade the Franks from marching against the enemy because he feared that they would seize all Syria if they were victorious, or, if they were defeated, the Sultan would seize his principality of Damascus.'[5] In the event Roger of Antioch crushed the sultan's army at Tell Danith on 14 September 1115, a battle which ended the sultan's interventions in Syria.

On the face of it, the withdrawal of Baghdad should have weakened the Islamic reaction to the western incursion, especially as the settlers adopted a fairly pragmatic attitude to dealing with their Muslim neighbours. Even before they reached Jerusalem the leaders of the First Crusade were happy to make arrangements with Muslims in areas outside their immediate concern. The western settlers were far from fanatical, understanding the importance of exploiting Muslim divisions. After a major attempt to conquer

Damascus failed in 1128, Jerusalem concluded a pact with the city for the joint exploitation of the Golan Heights. Its Burid rulers were happy to seek Christian support against threatening encroachments from other Muslim powers. Truces between Aleppo and its Christian neighbours were frequent, while there is ample evidence of some friendship and tolerance between the upper classes of the contending sides and sometimes this led to alliances across the religious divide. Yet that divide remained fundamental to the politics of the Middle East, as William of Tyre, who was born and lived in the Latin kingdom, recognized:

> War is waged differently and less vigorously between men who hold the same law and faith. For even if no other cause for hatred exists, the fact that the combatants do not share the same articles of faith is sufficient reason for constant quarrelling and enmity.[6]

The existence of this ideological hatred provided the basis for resistance which was fostered also by changing political circumstances. The cities of Syria had long been neglected because of the centrality of Iraq and Iran within the Arab and Turkish empires. But they remained prestigious and wealthy places and after 1115 independent Turkish lords saw these as theatres of ambition. In Damascus the Burids, descendants of its governor Tughtegin, played off their neighbours and cultivated their role as champions of the faith against the infidel. But the crucial city was Aleppo. After the death of Ridwan in 1113 there was political chaos. The citizens, frustrated by the failures of the sultans of Baghdad to render effective aid, turned to the warlike Turkish emirs of the nearby Jazira[7] for help.

In 1117 they appealed to Ilghazi of Mardin who took power on behalf of Ridwan's sons in 1118.[8] Ilghazi had as often allied with the Franks as he had fought them, but after his accession to power in Aleppo he seems to have cultivated a sense of *jihad*. In 1119 he gathered a great army against Antioch and in its ranks there were many holy men.[9] This force destroyed Roger of Antioch and his whole army at the 'Field of Blood' in 1119. It is a mark of the intense religious feelings aroused that almost all the prisoners were massacred. One of them, Robert FitzFulk, was paraded before his captors who demanded, 'Renounce your law, or die!', but he responded, 'I renounce all the works of Satan and his vices, I do not renounce dying for Christ' and was promptly decapitated.[10] Ilghazi lacked the power to mount sustained pressure upon Antioch, and after his death a series of emirs joined the power struggle within Aleppo which ended only when the sultan appointed Zengi, his governor of Mosul, to rule the city. Zengi had extensive territories already, and he came from a distinguished Aleppan family. So for the first time Aleppo was ruled by a powerful man who could claim a real legitimacy which he reinforced by marrying a Seljuq princess.

Zengi was a brutal tyrant. He meddled in the affairs of Baghdad, and established a supremacy over the tribes of the Jazira who provided him with excellent Turcomen fighters. In Syria he aimed to annexe Damascus but the city resisted all his efforts. In the pursuit of his ambitions Zengi fought Muslims almost as much as Franks and Byzantines. In 1144 Count Joscelin II of Edessa allied himself with Zengi's enemies in the Jazira, and when he took his army to their aid, Zengi mobilized his own forces and, after a siege of one month, seized Edessa, massacring the entire Latin population. Zengi had already started to portray himself as a champion of Islam. An inscription of 1138 on a Damascus *madrasa* (religious college) declares him to be 'the fighter of jihad, the defender of the frontier, the tamer of polytheists and the destroyer of heretics'.[11] The capture of Edessa made this a credible claim. Zengi was a ruthless Turkish soldier, but he needed the expertise of the city administrators and the support of the Arab notables who controlled the wealth of the cities in which they lived. *Jihad* was a way of reconciling them to his rule, of solidifying Sunni resistance to the threat of the western settlers and the siren calls of the Shi'ites, notably the Assassins who had been so influential in Syria.

The fall of Edessa in 1144 prompted Pope Eugene III (1145–53) to issue a call for the Second Crusade by the bull *Quantum Praedecessores* on 1 December 1145. The response to this appeal was at first lukewarm. Crusading and crusaders commanded respect, but England was enmeshed in a civil war during the reign of King Stephen (1135–54), while the succession of Conrad III of Germany (1137–52) was bitterly contested. In Italy the cities were pursuing their usual vendettas against one another. Moreover, Europeans had got used to the Holy Land defending itself for there had been no serious requests for help since 1128 when Baldwin II of Jerusalem needed troops to support his attempted conquest of Damascus. However, Louis VII of France (1137–80) was eager to go on crusade, and once he had enlisted the immense personal influence of Bernard of Clairvaux, the foremost spiritual leader of the day and later venerated as a saint, French and northern European aristocrats flocked to join him. Eventually even Conrad III was persuaded to join. Under the influence of three such stars of the European firmament two enormous armies gathered about Louis and Conrad and prepared to depart for the East. The presence of two kings in a crusading army was a remarkable testimony to the religious devotion of European people, as was the sheer size of their forces. Although the pope permitted some crusaders to discharge their vows by fighting in Spain and in eastern Germany, the huge German army may have between 30,000 and 35,000 strong though Louis VII's force was smaller. Other groups travelled independently, such as those that accompanied the count of Toulouse, Alfonso-Jordan, by sea. In addition, a substantial fleet of nearly 200 ships, carrying perhaps 12,000–15,000 troops and sailors from the Netherlands and England, set out for the Mediterranean, but were delayed because en route they besieged and captured Lisbon from the Muslims of Spain.[12] In total something like 70,000 set off.

The French arranged to follow the Germans down the Danube valley. Both made good time especially as the Germans left in situ their prefabricated bridges. However, neither king handled relations with the Byzantine empire very well, and as a result they received minimal help as they crossed its lands. In addition, the two kings had made no arrangements for cooperation beyond Constantinople, so Conrad set off into Anatolia alone. Neither Conrad nor Louis was a very competent general, so that despite all the fervour of the participants they suffered defeats in Anatolia which severely depleted their armies, only a rump of which ever reached the East.

Things went from bad to worse when they arrived in the Holy Land. In March 1147 Louis VII, after a hard march across Anatolia, received a splendid welcome at Antioch whose prince, Raymond of Poitiers, suggested that they join him in an attack on Aleppo. This was somewhat disconcerting to the newcomers because Louis and his leading men had come to reconquer Edessa. In fact all the Frankish leaders in the East were convinced that it was lost beyond redemption. And the campaign against Aleppo envisaged by Prince Raymond offered opportunities. In 1146 Zengi had been assassinated, and his son, Nur ad-Din's rule over a notoriously volatile city was precarious. However, Louis was unreceptive to the idea, preferring to press on to Jerusalem. The atmosphere between him and Prince Raymond was further poisoned by rumours that Queen Eleanor, who had accompanied her husband on crusade, had improper relations with Raymond who was her uncle. Raymond felt deserted and betrayed by Louis, and refused any further participation in events. Louis then enraged another important magnate of the Latin East, Raymond II, count of Tripoli, by refusing him military assistance. Raymond II was further alienated from the crusade by the arrival of Alfonso-Jordan, count of Toulouse, the legitimate son of Raymond IV of Toulouse, founder of the county of Tripoli, who, it was feared, might raise a claim to be count of Tripoli. When Alfonso-Jordan died suddenly, rumours of poisoning implicated Raymond II who was so angry that he refused to participate in the crusade.

Louis's co-crusader, Conrad III of Germany, had brought what was left of his army by sea from Constantinople so he was in Jerusalem well before the French king. In discussion with Baldwin III and his nobles in May, Conrad was persuaded to support an attack on Damascus. This city had for a long time been friendly to Jerusalem which it saw as an ally against the threatening power of Zengi. But because Nur ad-Din seemed to be weak it had recently allied with him against Jerusalem. This was an important reorientation of policy, and it undoubtedly prompted the nobles of Jerusalem to reverse their long-standing policy of friendship with Damascus. With an expedition to Edessa ruled out, Conrad III and Louis VII, as strangers to the East, had little option but to agree. The expedition, after some hard fighting, failed, probably because of determined resistance by Damascus and news that help was coming from the northern Muslims under Nur ad-Din whose prestige rose greatly as a result of his efforts. It is likely that to ensure their rapid departure the city offered some payment to the nobles of Jerusalem, and that this led the western crusaders to believe that treachery had led to their defeat. William of Tyre, the great historian of the Latin East who was himself a native of the kingdom, commented on the poisonous consequences of this debacle:

> The pilgrim princes therefore took counsel with one another. All too clearly they now perceived the treachery of those to whose loyalty they had entrusted their lives and interests and abhorred the perfidy by which they had been deceived. Convinced that their undertaking had no chance of success, they determined to abandon it and return home. Thus because of our sins, the kings and princes who had gathered in untold numbers were compelled to retreat without accomplishing their purpose. Covered with confusion and fear, they returned to the kingdom over the same road by which they had come. Henceforward, as long as they remained in the Orient, and, indeed, ever after, they looked askance on all the ways of our leaders.... Not only was this true in regard to themselves, but their influence caused others who had not been present to slacken in love toward the kingdom. As a result fewer people, and those less fervent in spirit, undertook this pilgrimage thereafter. Moreover, even to the present day, those who do come fear lest they be caught in the same toils and hence make as short a stay as possible.[13]

The whole sorry episode of the Second Crusade reveals something of the limitations of the crusade and of the Latin settlers in the East. The undoubted fervour triggered by St Bernard was not accompanied by any overarching organization. The French and German armies failed to work together, and even took separate routes across Anatolia, while both suffered from indiscipline, which was a factor in their defeats. Moreover, the military competence which characterized the leaders of the First Crusade was a serendipitous factor which did not reappear in 1147. When the crusaders finally got to the East the rulers of the western settlements welcomed them only in so far as they might lend aid to their own dynastic and territorial ambitions. But for crusaders, fired by ideology to undertake the difficult and dangerous fighting journey to the East, temporizing—and even negotiations with the Muslims—was difficult to understand. At Damascus, once the initial success was over, it was natural for the settlers to come to an agreement and to withdraw to fight another day. They had to think of the next time. But for the crusaders this seemed like treachery. It is hardly surprising, therefore, that despite many appeals for help, no major crusading expedition left Europe before the Battle of Hattin.

And this was the more perilous because of changes in the Islamic world. As the western army approached Damascus, prayers and ceremonies were said in the great mosque. The defenders were determined, reinforced by outsiders, and led by holy men some of whom were killed in the initial fighting:

> The army from Damascus had large numbers of auxiliaries; experienced Turkish storm-troopers, the citizen militia and volunteers fighting for the Faith. After a fierce struggle the Franks, superior in numbers and equipment, overwhelmed the Muslims, seized the water supplies and encamped in the gardens surrounding the city. They closed in on the city walls, coming up closer than any army in ancient or modern times had ever been. On this day the Malikite lawyer and scholar, the imam Yusuf al-Findalawi—God have mercy on him!—fell in battle, a martyr for the Faith, by the river at ar-Rabwa. He was facing the enemy and refusing to withdraw, in obedience to the precepts of God Almighty in His noble Book. The devout 'Abd ar-Rahman al-Halhuli met the same fate.

## As the siege developed

> cavalry and infantry from the province poured into the area. In the morning, reinforced and heartened, the Muslims returned to the battle. They stood firm and sent clouds of arrows from long-bows and cross-bows to rain down on the enemy's cavalry and infantry, horses and camels. That day a large detachment of archers arrived on foot from the Biqa', increasing the number of defenders and doubling their supply of arms.[14]

This formidable resistance owed much to the spirit of *jihad* and, combined with help from the Zengids of Aleppo, was enough to drive off the Second Crusade. This was a lesson which the new champion of Islam, Nur ad-Din, was to learn all too well.

There was nothing inevitable about the rise of Nur ad-Din. His position was at first far from secure and he had many enemies in the Muslim world. But he capitalized on his prestige from the defeat of the Second Crusade to agree an alliance with Unur, ruler of Damascus, and together they attacked Inab in the principality of Antioch. Raymond of Antioch marched to the relief of Inab, but with a small force, perhaps only 1,400, which Nur ad-Din's 6,000 totally destroyed, killing Prince Raymond on 29 June 1149.

This victory seems to have convinced Nur ad-Din that he was God's instrument, and after this time he adopted the title *mujahid*, 'warrior of the holy war', and began to wage a propaganda war proclaiming *jihad* against the western settlers and the Shi'ites, and especially against the Assassins whom he persecuted. Nur ad-Din took care to present himself as a pious Muslim, but more importantly he systematically adapted new religious institutions to his purpose. He lavished patronage on the new class of professional scholars and religious leaders which was emerging, providing them with study centres, most notably the colleges, *madrasas*, where Sunni law was taught. He was friendly to the Sufis whose mystical and esoteric form of Islam was becoming immensely popular. The construction of hospitals—like that at Damascus—mosques, and other religious buildings was a testament to his piety. In return the scholars propagated his image as the pious champion of true Islam, leading the *jihad* against the European settlers and Shi'ite heretics alike. In this way the fissiparous populations of the great Arab cities could be united in the cause of their Turkish overlords.

Of course, Nur ad-Din was no less personally ambitious than his father and many earlier Turkish warlords, and he spent much time fighting fellow Muslims. But he established a new style of Islamic leadership which radically changed the temper of the war against the Latin settlers in the Holy Land. Moreover, he shrewdly exalted the authority of the caliph of Baghdad whose influence was strengthening as the Seljuq sultans of Baghdad weakened, especially after 1153. In practice Nur ad-Din's immediate objective was Damascus at which he directed much of his propaganda. Gradually he won over opinion there. In January 1153, after long preparations, Baldwin III took advantage of the weakness of Fatimid Egypt to besiege Ascalon, the last Egyptian fortress in Palestine. The siege lasted until late August. The kingdom was so exhausted that it could not intervene and in April 1154 Damascus capitulated to Nur ad-Din. As a symbol of his power and of his concern for the city Nur ad-Din built a great *muristan* (hospital), though this was only one of his many foundations within the city, all of which represented Zengid propaganda.

When Nur ad-Din acquired control of both Aleppo and Damascus, he created an entirely new political and religious situation. The

European settlers could no longer play off Damascus against Aleppo. Control of all Syria was now vested in an able ruler who saw himself, and was increasingly seen, as the champion of Islam. This eminence gave him wide influence in the Islamic world far beyond what he ruled already. And that was very considerable, enabling him to support a substantial core army of some 6,000 well-armed and trained warriors who could be reinforced by more troops from the Jazira and the steppe, provided he could afford to pay them. This meant that at least occasionally he could raise armies of the order of 15,000. Baldwin III of Jerusalem responded to this new threat by an alliance with the Byzantine emperor Manuel Comnenus (1143–80).

The Byzantines wanted to dominate Anatolia and to reconquer the lands of the Turkish sultanate of Iconium at its very heart. The princes of Antioch were nominally vassals of the empire, but they had always resisted any expansion of its power because it would limit their freedom. After Raymond of Antioch's death at Inab in 1149, his son Bohemond III was a child, and his regent, Reynald of Châtillon, was captured by the Muslims in 1160 and imprisoned until 1176. The principality, therefore, needed Byzantine protection and had to agree to the alliance which gave Manuel considerable power in its internal affairs. This limited Nur ad-Din's freedom of action in north Syria. However, by the death of Baldwin III and the accession of Amalric I (1163–74), a serious crisis in Egypt was gripping the eastern Mediterranean, the resolution of which would form a vital part of the context of Hattin.

The Fatimid caliphate of Cairo had originally aspired to universal authority in Islam by spreading its Shi'ite faith, but by the mid-twelfth century factional struggles and scandals had discredited it even amongst Shi'ites. Increasingly the Fatimids were seen simply as the rulers of a purely Egyptian state where they had to share their authority with various court factions who struggled to appoint the vizier or chief minister. Moreover, the rise of Islamic *jihad* under Zengi and Nur ad-Din undermined their position even in Egypt which had always had a Sunni majority. The leaders of the Sunni were excluded from power by the members of the court circle around the caliph who often used Christians, drawn from the Coptic minority, as administrators. It is hardly surprising that Nur ad-Din's Sunni propaganda found important followers. Moreover, the regiments of the Fatimid army were recruited from many peoples, and the ethnic tension between them resulted in competition for resources. Quite naturally the regiments allied with court factions, and by the 1160s the leaders of the Sudanese infantry were particularly aggressive in their demands for pre-eminence, and fully prepared to throw military power behind their friends at court. These internal Egyptian struggles became 'internationalized' after 1162.

In that year a coup terminated the rule of the Ruzzik family who had imposed a degree of stability in Egypt in the late 1150s. In 1163 King Amalric of Jerusalem attacked Egypt seeking to enforce payment of the tribute of 33,000 dinars agreed by Ibn Ruzzik. Though their siege of the city of Bilbeis failed, the expedition revealed the weakness of Egypt. Competing factions in Egypt now appealed to either Nur ad-Din or Amalric for support. In 1164 Nur ad-Din sent his Kurdish general, Shirkuh, to invade Egypt and he imposed one Shawar as vizier. But Shawar, to assure his independence, called in Amalric, king of Jerusalem, paying him the extraordinary sum of 400,000 dinars. For the moment the two powers cancelled one another out and both left Egypt. But each could count on support from factions within the country, and in

1166 Shirkuh came again, but was forced to retreat by a combined Jerusalemite/Fatimid force, and once more Shawar was left in control of Egypt.

In 1167 the internationalization of the Egyptian crisis widened. King Amalric married Manuel's great-grand-niece, Maria Comnena, and agreed an alliance to seize Egypt. However, in 1168 Amalric decided not to await Byzantine help, presumably because he did not wish to divide the spoils of conquest, and launched an outright attempt to conquer Egypt. Shawar again appealed to Nur ad-Din who once more sent Shirkuh. The Syrian–Egyptian alliance managed to defeat Amalric, but Shirkuh then turned on and killed Shawar, taking control of Egypt in the name of Nur ad-Din. Amalric failed because he rejected the support of factions loyal to the Fatimids, and compounded the failure by not waiting for the Byzantines. Amalric had invested very heavily in the success of his Egyptian expedition and was impoverished by its failure. The Hospital, which had backed him to the hilt, was bankrupted by their participation. Significantly, the Templars had refused to join any of these Egyptian adventures: like so many of the territorial powers of the settler East, the orders put their own interest before ideological ends.

Shirkuh now assumed the position of Fatimid vizier, but he died on 22 March 1169 and his clever nephew, Saladin, now seized control of Egypt. For reasons which are unclear to us Nur ad-Din had a deep suspicion of Saladin. This distrust increased when Saladin, aware of the precarious nature of his position in Egypt, refused to abolish the Fatimid caliphate. Although many of the civil servants of the Fatimid regime had rallied to his cause, the caliph and his court remained influential and enjoyed the devoted support of the 30,000 African troops of the Egyptian army. In

August 1069, provoked by Saladin's hostility to the caliph, they rebelled, precipitating a savage struggle for survival. The 'white' troops who formed the cavalry of the Fatimid army stood aloof, but in the streets of Cairo the black infantry were very effective against Saladin's relatively small forces. Saladin ruthlessly attacked their wives and children and massacred the black soldiers as they tried to defend their families. In 1169 Saladin fought off a joint Byzantine and Jerusalemite attack on Egypt, enhancing his prestige, and this enabled him to depose the Fatimid caliph in 1171. In that year Amalric and Manuel projected another attack on Egypt but it took time to materialize.

Saladin had risen to power by adroitly exploiting the divisions of his enemies, but Nur ad-Din distrusted him and he feared elements of the former Fatimid regime might ally with Jerusalem or Byzantium against him. However, fortune favoured Saladin, because in 1174 Nur ad-Din died, leaving only children as his heirs. Almost immediately Amalric also died and the child, Baldwin IV (1174–85), who succeeded him suffered from leprosy. Succession crises, therefore, afflicted both Muslim Syria and Christian Jerusalem.

Saladin had ruthlessly destroyed his enemies in Egypt, but in assuming power he had clothed himself in an aura of piety, pledging himself to an austere life and giving lavish support to holy men. He proclaimed his devotion to Sunni Islam and its leaders, the Abbasid caliphs at Baghdad. The caliphs, profiting from the collapse of the Seljuq dynasty in 1153, were glad to enjoy the recognition of a powerful Islamic ruler and in return could give his pretensions a useful legitimacy. And as the heads of Sunni Islam they were pleased to endorse his devotion to the *jihad* against dissident Muslims and the westerners who held Jerusalem.

In practice Saladin did not at first do much against the Franks beyond some skirmishing and raids in Jerusalemite territory. But his defeat of the attack in 1169 and of a renewed Byzantine assault on Alexandria in July 1174 had enhanced his prestige. In Damascus various factions struggled for power in the name of Nur ad-Din's young son, As-Salih Ismail al-Malik, and on 28 October 1174 some of the leading soldiers handed the citadel of Damascus over to him as the guardian and protector of the child. This infuriated the boy's family, the Zengids, who controlled Mosul and Aleppo where the young child took refuge, but they were not strong enough to evict Saladin from Damascus. Despite his oft-proclaimed devotion to the holy war Saladin spent much time and energy in fighting against Muslim enemies, especially the Zengid family, and it was not until 1183 that he finally seized Aleppo, completing the union of Syria and Egypt.

This union was clearly an enormous accretion of strength for Saladin. The western settlers were quite pragmatic in their attitudes to Muslim powers, but the rise of *jihad*, which was vital to Saladin's whole position, meant there was little chance of an accommodation with their neighbours. At the same time the kingdom of Jerusalem was experiencing grave internal conflicts. It has often been thought, therefore, that its ultimate destruction was inevitable. But this is perfect hindsight. Saladin had problems of his own. In acquiring more lands he also added more enemies, while the internal political quarrels of the western settlers, which figure so prominently in accounts of this period, could easily have been ended by a turn of fate. Saladin had secured Damascus, but the Zengid family retained control of Aleppo where they guarded Nur ad-Din's son, As-Salih Ismail al-Malik. He was as yet a child, but there could be no doubt that he was his father's true heir. This was a grave threat to Saladin's hold on Damascus, and As-Salih's claims enjoyed the support of the Zengid family in Mosul and elsewhere. In 1174 Saladin and the Zengids prepared for war, and both sides made peace with the Latin kingdom in order to clear the way for their conflict.

In fact Saladin negotiated with the Zengids, pretending to seek a settlement, but he drew their army into battle near the Orontes Gorges on 13 April 1175 and won a great victory. However, Aleppo held out for the young As-Salih, and Saladin accepted this by a formal treaty. By 1176 they were fighting again. Saladin concluded a truce with the Latin kingdom which left him free to pursue the war. On 22 April 1176 he crushed the Zengids and their allies at the Battle of Tell al-Sultan. However, the Zengids still held Aleppo and Mosul, while Saladin's army was becoming tired. At this point the leaders of the Latin kingdom, conscious of the danger posed by Saladin's success, raided Damascene territory, forcing Saladin to accept Zengid control of Aleppo. The Zengids were divided amongst themselves, but Saladin was very conscious that once he reached his majority As-Salih would provide them with a threatening rallying point. Before he returned to Damascus, Saladin attacked the Assassins in their stronghold of Masyaf in the southern Nusairi mountains. Alarmed by Saladin's success, they had sought to preserve the balance of power in Syria by killing him during his attack on Aleppo. The attempt failed, but Saladin's response, an assault on their great stronghold of Masyaf, went badly and in the meantime his troops defending Damascus were crushed by Baldwin IV of Jerusalem (1174–85) at the Battle of Ain al-Jarr. Saladin then proceeded via Damascus to Egypt because he needed to watch his frontier with Sudan in the south, to maintain Egyptian influence in the Yemen, and to protect the Holy Places in Arabia.

Throughout the conflict with the Zengids and their allies Saladin was obliged to tread warily. As the self-proclaimed leader of Islam against the western unbelievers he had to counter the obvious fact that he was waging war on the legitimate ruler of the Zengid lands. He was careful to impress the professional administrators and religious leaders in the Arab cities by ostentatious piety and patronage of Islamic institutions. He also lavished praise upon the caliphs at Baghdad who were in the process of rebuilding their military power after the eclipse of the Seljuq sultans of Baghdad in 1153. But while the caliphs were delighted to have this kind of support, their cause was best served by playing off Saladin against the Zengids and so they could often be cool to anything which upset the balance. Moreover, as the self-proclaimed champion of Islam, Saladin was asking to be judged by the highest standards, yet his treaties with the Europeans opened him to charges of hypocrisy. His religious pretentions and extensive lands imposed wide responsibilities.

Therefore any view of the warfare in the Middle East as simply pitting the western settlers against Saladin is a dramatic simplification, for if he made war against one enemy, another could rise against him. Moreover, although Saladin's empire appears enormous on the map, its nature needs to be considered. Essentially he depended upon numerous governors and warlords who, by one title or another, actually controlled the machinery of state in their areas. Their allegiance to him was always conditional and dependent upon him recognizing their interests. Thus he could not easily mobilize the resources of his vast lands. Everything depended upon the interplay between local circumstances and concerns and Saladin's personal prestige at any given moment. His championing of *jihad* was, of course, of great significance but far from all-important in his relations with his nominal subordinates.

And then there was the problem of the army. The professional element in the army was made up of brilliantly effective soldiers. They fought as horse archers but were increasingly well equipped to fight the Franks at close quarters. However, only the core troops, for the most part Kurds or Turks who had campaigned with him in Egypt, were closely tied to Saladin. The remainder, mostly Turkish, were always in a sense allies brought by the local notables who had submitted conditionally to his rule. They were excellent soldiers, but there was a limit to what they could be asked to do, and especially to how long they could be kept in the field, because like all soldiers, in the end they needed to go home to supervise the farms which provided their basic income. And if there was no loot forthcoming, soldiers would flag and ultimately refuse to fight. As well as the professionals, Saladin could fill his ranks with paid men, like the Arabs, the Bedouin, and others, mostly serving as light cavalry, who had much the same basic limitations as the professionals, but whose discipline and cohesion were markedly inferior. Of course, he could count on religious volunteers, but their numbers and expertise are uncertain. Great as his resources were, Saladin could not support a large standing army for long periods of time. And he had to face the uncertainties of war, for after all,

> War is the realm of chance. No other human activity gives it greater scope; no other has such incessant and varied dealings with this intruder. Chance makes everything more uncertain and interferes with the whole course of events.[15]

And one of the greatest of these random factors was military leadership. A good general could inspire an army, while a bad one could bring ruination. Simple mistakes have serious consequences in war, and if Saladin made them, his whole empire could be at stake. Prestige, and especially military prestige, was the slender thread on which Saladin's power hung. The same, of course, applied to the Frankish states, and although they were very small, their position was far from hopeless and they possessed great military strength, as the events of 1177 clearly demonstrated.

In that year, buoyed up by his victories over the Zengids and his rising prestige, Saladin resolved to reinforce his image as the champion of Islam by attacking the kingdom of Jerusalem. He knew that many of the kingdom's knights were in the principality of Antioch to support an attack on Aleppo, made possible by the presence on crusade of a major western potentate, Count Philip of Flanders. Saladin gathered a great army and invaded from Egypt, passing Ascalon on 23 November. It was much too late in the season for a serious attack on any of the cities of the kingdom, and in any case his army does not seem to have been carrying siege equipment, so his purpose was probably to spread destruction in the enemy heartlands. He perhaps assumed that as Baldwin IV of Jerusalem was a child and a leper he could enjoy an easy success which would raise his prestige in the Muslim world, counter the effects of the defeat at Ain al-Jarr, and reassert his claim to be the champion of Islam. Saladin's large army invaded the southern part of the kingdom from Egypt. It was so numerous that Baldwin IV, conscious that the Aleppo expedition had reduced his forces, withdrew behind the walls of Ascalon, allowing Saladin's main force to proceed into the core of the kingdom unchallenged. But whatever Saladin may have hoped to achieve, he was soon to come face to face with reality.

The strength of the kingdom of Jerusalem lay in the walled cities, any one of which could be taken only by a major siege. But an invading army which stopped to besiege a city would be subject to attack by the field army of the kingdom, which could count on close knowledge of the area and active support from the numerous castles which studded the countryside and served as centres of supply and support. And the field army of Jerusalem was formidable. At its heart were the barons and knights of the kingdom, some 600 heavily armed cavalrymen who were experienced soldiers accustomed to working together in the constant warfare which afflicted the kingdom. They were supported by 5,000–6,000 foot soldiers from amongst the general settler population, many of whom were also veterans. In addition, it was possible to hire mercenary troops as both cavalry and infantry. The royal army could also count on the help of the two great religious orders of the Hospital and the Temple who could each put into the field about 300 knights together with their own light cavalry or turcopoles, and infantry. They too could hire mercenaries to enhance their forces. As always with medieval armies it is difficult to estimate how large an army could be raised by the Latin kingdom, but for the campaign of Hattin, as we shall see, a massive effort created an army of about 18,000 which included 1,200 knights. By contemporary standards this was an enormous force. In 1214 the king of France confronted an allied army led by the German emperor in a battle at Bouvines which settled the shape of European politics for generations to come, yet each side had only 1,200 knights and 6,000–7,000 foot.

The army which took shelter in Ascalon was probably much smaller than the kingdom could have raised by a maximum effort, partly because of the Antioch expedition and partly because Saladin had moved very quickly. The settlers had no way of knowing Saladin's intentions and may have assumed he was aiming to seize some important target, perhaps even Jerusalem itself. Baldwin IV was at this time only 15, and effective control of the army was vested in Reynald of Châtillon, lord of Kerak who gained great prestige from what followed. Saladin's force may well have been dispersed for ravaging but it was clearly very large. The army of Jerusalem, despite being heavily outnumbered, was, however, determined to precipitate a battle because they feared that Saladin might attack Jerusalem.

Baldwin moved northward, passed close to Saladin's main force, and trailed his coat in order to tempt Saladin to pursue them. In fact Baldwin's purpose was to draw Saladin onto unfavourable ground and in this he succeeded brilliantly. The battle took place on 25 November 1177 near to a hill called Montgisart, which is usually identified with Tel Gezer, about 8 kilometres south-east of Ramla. Here Saladin found himself close to the Judaean Hills amidst marshy ground cut by streams; this was a very unsuitable situation for his army whose great strength was rapid and fluid manoeuvre. However, it favoured the settlers whose heavy cavalry excelled at close-quarter fighting. The battle was savage: the Hospital in Jerusalem reportedly treated 2,000 injured from their own side. But Saladin's army suffered very heavy losses, was scattered and largely destroyed, and indeed, its leader was lucky to escape with his life as the remnants fled across the desert to Egypt. Montgisart was an unpleasant and unexpected defeat for Saladin, and for the next few years, although he won some notable victories, his stance with regard to the settler kingdom was essentially defensive.

While Saladin was preoccupied in shoring up his battered prestige, Baldwin IV went on the offensive. In October 1178 he began the construction of a castle at Jacob's Ford which controlled a major crossing of the Jordan and therefore could serve as a base for attacks on Damascus, and gave it to the Templars. Saladin was so alarmed by this very evident threat to Damascus that he offered Baldwin 100,000 dinars to halt the building operations; this was refused. In early 1179 Baldwin led a raid onto the Golan Heights, only to suffer heavy losses, amongst them a great lord, Humphrey of Toron. In May 1179 Saladin attacked Jacob's Ford but was repulsed by the garrison and his army moved northwards into the Beqaa valley. Emboldened, Baldwin IV pursued them and his cavalry fell upon and destroyed advanced elements of Saladin's army. In the process they far outstripped their own infantry who were unable to help when they in turn were attacked and scattered by the main enemy force. Baldwin, unable to mount a horse because of his illness, was carried off by one of his knights and saved by his bodyguard who hacked a way through the enemy. The Battle of Marj Ayun cost Baldwin many casualties, but its worst consequences soon followed.

Confident in the knowledge that he had mauled his enemy badly, Saladin promptly marched on Jacob's Ford, starting the siege of the castle on 25 August. Although the castle was incomplete it had a large garrison and offered fierce resistance, sustained by the hope of early relief. From the steep hillside on the east bank of the Jordan, Muslim archers kept up a shower of arrows, while Saladin's sappers strove to undermine its northern wall, suffering very heavy losses. Saladin, fearful that Baldwin would raise a relief army, offered his men rich rewards to press the attack. His sappers breached the castle walls and his army stormed through the gap in overwhelming numbers and massacred the garrison. Their corpses, some 700 in number, were dumped in a cistern. Shortly after, perhaps as a result of contact with bodies from the garrison, disease ravaged Saladin's army, killing ten important emirs. Syria had been suffering from a drought and in Egypt the Nile flood had failed several years running and undoubtedly these were factors which drove Saladin to a treaty with Jerusalem in 1180. William of Tyre considered the terms 'humble enough on our part', probably meaning that Baldwin IV had not extracted tribute from the Muslims. Raymond III of Tripoli initially refused to agree to the truce, but was forced to in the end by a series of devastating Muslim raids on the county of Tripoli. However, Saladin had preoccupations in the Muslim world, notably with the threat posed to his influence in the north by Kilij Arslan of Rhum and the possibilities opened by the death of Saif ad-Din Ghazi II (1170–80), the Zengid ruler of Mosul. Saladin gained little from his exertions in this area and returned to Egypt where internal disputes preoccupied him until news came of the death on 4 December 1181 of As-Salih of Aleppo. Had this son of Nur ad-Din lived to full manhood he would have been a formidable rival to Saladin, and his death must be accounted a stroke of luck, although Saladin achieved little in the short run because the Zengids seized control of Aleppo.

Thus far Saladin, mindful of his defeat in 1177, had acted purely defensively in regard to the Latins, but he was clearly emboldened by his recent victories and spurred onto the offensive by the need to strengthen public perception of his role as champion of Islam. He may have been encouraged also by events in Byzantium. In 1180 the emperor Manuel Comnenus died, leaving a child as his heir. In 1182 Andronicus Comnenus was able to mount a coup, riding a wave of anti-Latin feeling to make himself emperor (1182–5). Thus Jerusalem had no ally in the eastern Mediterranean. In 1182 Saladin renounced the treaty with Jerusalem, nominally in response to a raid on a caravan by Reynald of Châtillon. His great fortress of Kerak was the centre of the Latin lordship of Outre-Jourdain, the fertile rim of land to the east of the Dead Sea extending from south of modern Amman to Petra. This enabled its holder to dominate the trade route between Egypt and Damascus and to extort tribute from passing caravans.

It was bad enough that the Franks could exert pressure upon communications between these two parts of Saladin's empire, but the aggressive attitudes of Reynald of Châtillon added a new dimension. This western lord had come to the East on the Second Crusade, married Constance of Antioch, and ruled that principality from 1153 until 1160 when he was captured on a ravaging expedition. He was held in prison at Aleppo until 1176 when, on his release, he took for his wife Stephanie, the heiress to the lordship of Outre-Jourdain. Reynald was a formidable soldier who had played a major role at Montgisart and later, in an act deeply threatening to Saladin's prestige, attacked the pilgrim routes to Mecca.

After renouncing the peace Saladin besieged Kerak, but he could not sustain the siege because of the arrival of the army of Jerusalem. However, the Latins did not attack him and he set off north and on 12 July he encamped on the Jordan to the south of the Sea of Galilee. On 13 July he sent forces against Beit She'an (then Baisan). Syrian reinforcements had brought his army up to some 20,000, which William of Tyre describes as the largest force yet to have attacked the kingdom. The army of the kingdom had also marched north to concentrate at Saforie (ancient: Sepphoris, Hebrew: Tzippori, Arabic: Safurriya) where the remains of the ancient city, crowned by a small crusader castle, provided shelter, and copious springs offered a good water supply. Saladin, confident in numbers, seems to have been hoping to draw Baldwin IV's host into battle.

The army of the kingdom comprised only some 700 mounted men and an unknown number of infantry, but despite this it advanced aggressively against Saladin, marching into the Jordan valley and spending the night of 14 July on the hillside close to the Hospitaller castle of Belvoir. On 15 July they reached the plain between Baisan and Taiyiba, which in crusader times was called Forbelet, where Saladin tried to surround them. Despite constant and determined charges by Saladin's army, the Frankish host kept their formation and withdrew uphill to Forbelet. Saladin's army was exhausted by the battle and any attempt to penetrate further into the kingdom via the Jezreel valley would have been dangerous with the Latins threatening his flank, so he withdrew having achieved nothing. The army of the kingdom was extremely bold to close with such a massive force, yet it was hardly foolhardy. Their attack was supported by the two strong castles of Belvoir and Forbelet. Once Saladin had failed to crush them, he simply could not persist in his siege of Baisan because the Jerusalemite army was close enough to threaten his army. The great puzzle is who was in command? For although Baldwin had been at Saforie, in his account of the battle William of Tyre makes no mention of him and simply notes the impressive performance of certain nobles like Balian of Ibelin. Raymond of Tripoli, it is known, was ill at this time. It is quite possible that the king had been incapacitated by his leprosy, as was to happen increasingly often. Its onset may explain why the army of Jerusalem had failed to attack Saladin at Kerak, and why Baldwin was apparently absent from the fighting at Forbelet. It is not known, however, to whom he confided control of his army. What can be said, however, is that the aggressive actions of the Latins at Baisan bear all the hallmarks of the man who had triumphed at Montgisart.

Baldwin was active again by the next month, because he successfully drove off Saladin's carefully prepared land and sea assault against Beirut. This was a remarkable operation which reveals the scope of Saladin's ambitions. Egypt had once been the foremost naval power in the eastern Mediterranean, a real rival at sea to Byzantium. The Fatimids had tried to use their naval power against the western settlers, but they could not match the skills and maritime technology of the Italian city states whose fleets quickly dominated the Levant. Saladin invested heavily in new ships which he now put to good use. While his brother, al-Adil raided into the southern part of the kingdom from Egypt, the fleet moved up to Beirut about 1 August, and Saladin himself brought his forces across the Beqaa valley to besiege the city. The seizure of Beirut would have cut off Jerusalem from land communication with Tripoli and Antioch. Saladin's army apparently lacked machinery, but it tried to repeat the success of Jacob's Ford by undermining the walls under cover of a hail of arrows. However, the news that Baldwin was marching to relieve the city with the support of Christian ships forced Saladin to raise the siege. This assault on Beirut was an impressive indication of Saladin's growing military capacity. But the offensive campaigns of 1182 had actually achieved very little. The Muslim sources try to pretend that these were just raids, but the forces which Saladin had assembled suggest that he had had much more in mind.

Nonetheless the campaign of 1182 is important because Saladin had taken the offensive. The devastation he had inflicted was notable, while away from the main fighting some of his troops had taken the cave fortress of Habis Jaldak on the Yarmuk River. So, despite ultimate failure, Saladin could show some results. In any case the Muslim chroniclers were able to gloss over the limitations of his achievements because shortly after he enjoyed a stunning success, albeit against fellow Muslims. Zengid rule in Aleppo had become unpopular, partly because of divisions within the family, and Saladin moved into the Jazira to exploit their political problems in that area. While he was at pains to portray this as an effort to unite Islam against the infidel, none could miss the obvious fact that he was furthering his own ambitions by war against Muslims. Furthermore, during this campaign in the north the Franks regained Habis Jaldak. Then in 1183 Reynald of Châtillon staged a raid by sea and land into the Red Sea which actually at one stage threatened Medina where the Prophet was buried. Reynald's troops were quickly dealt with before they caused any real harm, but the whole episode scandalized Muslims and reflected poorly on Saladin himself. This is undoubtedly why he refused to honour the agreed surrender of 170 of the raiders and ordered their execution, while at the same time vowing to kill the raid's initiator, Reynald, at the first opportunity. In the meantime he continued the war with the Zengids and in June 1183 this culminated in the seizure of Aleppo despite the hostile attitude of its population. Saladin was now the master of all Syria, and his power extended into the Jazira, and so he prepared to resume the holy war. On 24 August he returned to Damascus and mustered a new army for the invasion of the kingdom of Jerusalem. On 29 September he again crossed the Jordan and sacked Baisan whose inhabitants had fled north to Tiberias. His blows fell upon a kingdom shaken by internal dissent.

# 3

# The Battle of Hattin

At the root of the crisis was Baldwin IV's leprosy. He was only 13 when his father died in 1174, and because of his youth a regent or *bailli* had to be appointed, and that was Raymond III of Tripoli. The county of Tripoli was independent of the kingdom of Jerusalem, but Raymond had acquired the important fief of Galilee, which was part of Jerusalem, by marriage to its widowed countess Eschiva. He was, therefore, one of the greatest lords of the kingdom. In addition, he was the nearest adult male relative of Baldwin IV. He commanded great respect amongst his peers and ruled the kingdom well until 1176 when Baldwin came of age. Yet it was obvious that the king would at times be incapacitated by his disease, would probably not live long, and most certainly would be unable to produce a male heir. For this reason, in 1176 his elder sister, Sybil, born of Amalric's first marriage to Agnes of Courtenay, was married to William 'Longsword' of Monferrat in Italy, a distinguished western magnate. Unfortunately William died very soon after, and, even more unfortunately, in 1177 Sybil gave birth to his child, the future Baldwin V, raising the prospect of a protracted regency in the event of Baldwin IV's death which was unlikely to be long delayed. Moreover, infants commonly died young in the kingdom. Therefore there was bound to be considerable concern about any further marriage which Sybil might make, for she was her brother's heir. Moreover, by his second wife, Maria Comnena, King Amalric had another daughter, Isabel, who could well be seen as having a claim.

All aristocracies were inevitably divided by factional struggles in which personal likes and dislikes played a major role. Such conflicts were about royal patronage—acquiring office, prestige, and profit, and preventing enemies from getting them—and they were rarely fatal to the state. Medieval government was intensely personal and, therefore, heavily dependent upon the randomness of survival and the vagaries of individual character. And such rivalries were commonly violent. In 1168 Guy of Lusignan ambushed and murdered Patrick, earl of Salisbury in pursuit of a family feud, and it may be as a result of this that he had fled from the wrath of Henry II of England and followed his elder brother, Amalric, to Jerusalem. But there were special factors that made disputes in the kingdom of Jerusalem particularly bitter.

The ruling circle within Jerusalem was very narrow, for there were only about thirty lordships, many of them very petty. Moreover, even the greatest, like Sidon and Arsuf, were not especially prosperous. Raymond's Galilee looks impressive, but within its territory were many ecclesiastical institutions which owed him no service, while there were extensive wastelands. His eminence really rested upon his county of Tripoli which stood outside the kingdom. The increasing intensity of warfare in the second half of the twelfth century further strained the resources of the lords. In its early years the kingdom extracted tribute from its Muslim neighbours, but as their threat became more dangerous so this source of income vanished, while all hope of territorial expansion seemed to have come to an end after Amalric's failure to seize Egypt by 1174. Worse still, as Saladin became stronger he was able to launch attacks into the very heart of the kingdom, and these must have been cruel blows to many.

A symptom of their problems was the sale by the great lords of land and castles to the military orders. For the most part, therefore, this was an aristocracy in difficulties, heavily dependent upon the king whose control of the more important cities gave him greater wealth and authority. The cities were trading centres which the king could tax. Trade was so important to both sides of the Muslim–Christian divide that it was allowed to continue even in times of war. But the aristocrats of the kingdom could only get access to this wealth through the generosity of the king. There was, therefore, tremendous competition to influence him and the arrival of new blood, like the Lusignan brothers, while needed was at the same time hardly welcome because they were also simply additional competitors for royal generosity. At the same time the orders were emerging as a new and disquieting political force. They were essential to the defence of the kingdom, yet responsible only to the pope and not to the king.

The military pressure exerted by Saladin underlined the insecurity of the kingdom. The barons of Jerusalem were not, for the most part, fanatics; they were categorically not crusaders in that sense. But they were fiercely and proudly Catholic and deeply aware of the dangers posed by their Muslim neighbours to their very existence. The sense of what they had to lose could only contribute to the sharpness of the differences over policy which divided them. As a whole they were quite prepared to deal peacefully with Muslims, but they were also aware that they needed to be seen to be strong, and that their position depended heavily on prestige and the assurance of victory. So the bitterness of political relations in the kingdom of Jerusalem was remarkable.

The uncertain situation of the monarchy in the late 1170s created a situation which greatly fostered such rivalries. Baldwin IV needed to assert his authority and he seems to have distrusted Raymond of Tripoli, his former *bailli*, whom he largely excluded from power, perhaps fearing his possible claim on the throne as his own nearest adult male relative. Instead he built up his own party, prominent amongst whom were his mother, Agnes of Courtenay, her brother Joscelin III of Courtenay, and Reynald of Châtillon. Associated with them were two brothers of the important baronial house of Lusignan in Poitou who were newcomers to the kingdom. Amalric, the elder, arrived first and though his marriage to Eschiva, a daughter of Baldwin of Ibelin, had entered court circles and become a favourite of Agnes of Courtenay. His younger brother Guy came to the East between 1173 and 1180. He quickly became so close to the widowed Sybil that rumours of a possible marriage between them were very soon circulating. Baldwin tried to arrange for Sybil to marry Hugh III of Burgundy, but the negotiations were inconclusive. The prospect of Guy, a mere newcomer, rising so high by marriage seems to have excited the opposition of some of the barons of the kingdom and this produced a crisis in 1180. Raymond of Tripoli, along with his close ally and relative, Bohemond III of Antioch, entered the kingdom in arms:

> This caused the king much alarm; for he feared that they might try to bring about a revolution, in which case, after dethroning him, they might try to seize the realm themselves. The king's malady was now troubling him more than ever, and from day to day the symptoms of leprosy became more and more apparent.[1]

Baldwin was able to outface the two great princes, who soon returned to their own lands, but he was probably uncertain of sustained support from the barons of the kingdom, amongst whom Raymond was very popular, so in haste at Easter 1180 he married Sybil to Guy, with whom she was infatuated. In consequence Guy immediately became count of Jaffa and Ascalon, but of course he also joined the royal circle and became a factor in the succession. This was not without merit: he was Baldwin's choice and the lords of Lusignan were important nobles in Poitou, and as a result had close connections to the kings of both France and England. Shortly after this, the patriarch of Jerusalem died. Baldwin declined to appoint William of Tyre, who was closely associated with Raymond of Tripoli, and instead chose Heraclius, a personal favourite of his mother Agnes. Tensions remained high, and when Raymond left Tripoli for his barony of Galilee Baldwin forbade him to re-enter the kingdom, perhaps fearing another coup like that attempted in 1180. The two were reconciled by the time of Saladin's attack in 1182, but Raymond's illness kept him out of the campaign of that year, and this could hardly have endeared him to Baldwin.

Saladin's acquisition of Aleppo was an obvious threat to the kingdom which, in February 1183, announced the levying of an extraordinary tax to pay for defence. Heraclius, patriarch of Jerusalem and William, archbishop of Tyre were charged with its collection. By late August Saladin was at Damascus, assembling a great army against Jerusalem. In response, Baldwin IV summoned the host of the kingdom which gathered, as in 1182, at Saforie. It was perhaps the biggest the kingdom had ever put into the field, with some 1,300 cavalry and 15,000 infantry. But the king became very ill, and on 17 August, in an assembly at nearby Nazareth, he made the barons swear obedience to Guy as his *bailli*. Command of the army, therefore, passed to this young Poitevin. In late September Saladin crossed the Jordan and sacked Baisan whose inhabitants had already fled to Tiberias, and then ravaged the Jezreel valley. In contrast to the previous year, Guy at first made no response and kept his army at Saforie. To avoid battle while keeping an army in being close to the attackers was not unreasonable because it prevented Saladin from attacking any major target. However, Saforie was so distant from the enemy force that the Muslims were able to disperse their troops safely and thereby do a great deal of damage. The contrast with the events of 1182, when an aggressive approach drove Saladin off, was patent. The inaction caused considerable unrest in the army, and probably as a result Guy marched south to La Fève (modern Afula) and proceeded beyond there to encamp at the springs of Ain Jalut and Ain Tuba'un. This was a fighting march, with the Latin infantry defending the cavalry from the arrows of the Muslim horse archers, and Saladin seems to have hesitated to block their approach lest he be exposed to a massive charge against his main force. For eight days Saladin tried to provoke the Jerusalemites into a battle but failed even to prevent the movement of food to their camp, and so withdrew. But there was considerable dissension within the Christian army

> through hatred of the count of Jaffa, to whom, two days before, the king had entrusted the welfare of the kingdom. For they took it ill that at so critical and dangerous a time matters of the highest importance had been placed in the hands of an obscure man, wholly incapable and indiscreet.[2]

As in 1182, Saladin had failed to precipitate a major battle, but he had ravaged an enormous stretch of countryside, inflicted considerable losses on Guy's army, and increased his own prestige.

In the kingdom the whole campaign was seen as a fiasco, and severe political consequences ensued. In fact King Baldwin mounted a coup from above. He stripped Guy of all offices in the presence of the leaders of the realm and insisted upon the coronation of his 5-year-old nephew, the child of Sybil and her dead husband William 'Longsword' of Monferrat, as Baldwin V. His clear intent was to bar Sybil from the succession because of her marriage. Guy defied the king and attacked the royal lands, but despite the urging of Heraclius the patriarch and the masters of the Hospital and Temple, Baldwin refused to readmit him to favour. In truth the king was intent on excluding Guy from the succession to the kingdom and attempted to annul his marriage to Sybil, who, however, seems to have been devoted to her husband.

In late 1183 Baldwin made Raymond of Tripoli his *bailli* and decreed that he was to remain in office until Baldwin V had reached majority, in the meantime enjoying control of Beirut to defray his expenses. It was perhaps because Raymond had a claim to the throne and might be accused of murder if the young king died, that care of the young Baldwin V was entrusted to Joscelin of Courtenay. His elevation may also have been a gesture to the friends of Guy with whom he had been associated. If Baldwin V died before his majority, Raymond of Tripoli was to continue in office as *bailli* until a committee of the pope and the kings of England and France had arbitrated between the claims of Sybil and her half-sister, Isabel. In his anxiety to exclude Guy, Baldwin IV was prepared to envisage the succession of Sybil's younger sister, Isabel, who in 1183 married one of the great nobles of the kingdom, Humphrey IV of Toron. The trouble with these elaborate arrangements was that in the event of Baldwin V's death they threatened to deny Sybil's rights. In an age when the hereditary principle was held sacred, any attempt to enforce this provision would inevitably raise doubts in the minds of the nobility whose own positions were based on inheritance. The best outcome, of course, would have been for Baldwin V to become king, but everyone knew that there was a strong possibility that he would die before he became an adult.

In 1184 Heraclius, along with Roger de Moulins, grand master of the Hospitallers and Arnold of Torroja, grand master of the Knights Templar (who died on the journey), travelled to Europe to seek assistance for the beleaguered kingdom of Jerusalem. They offered the crown to both Henry II of England and Philip Augustus of France, both of whom refused. This seems extraordinary in the light of the settlement already reached, but perhaps nobody fully believed in it. Heraclius and his companions must have had some warrant for approaching the two kings, so this indicates much uncertainty in ruling circles in Jerusalem. In the event they raised much money and some promises of troops for the kingdom. Most of those who had vowed to go on crusade arrived in 1186, only to discover that a truce had been concluded with Saladin—and so returned home disgruntled.

Raymond of Tripoli may have been *bailli*, but Baldwin IV continued to be active. In November 1183, in an effort to retrieve his reputation which had been sullied by the assault on Muslim Holy Places inspired by Reynald of Châtillon, Saladin attacked Kerak. He had a major army and an ample siege train. Reynald refused to allow the citizens of Kerak entry to the castle because he was determined to defend the town itself. However, his forces

were overrun by the mighty Muslim army and forced to fall back
into the fortress which was almost lost in the rush for safety.
Saladin set up seven catapults which bombarded the castle. There
was much confusion within because the attack had coincided
with the marriage there of Humphrey of Toron to Isabel, Baldwin's younger sister. It is said that Saladin chivalrously ordered
that the tower in which the young couple were housed should
not be bombarded. It is certainly true that the siege was not
pressed, and when the army of Jerusalem approached from
south of the Dead Sea, Saladin chose not to challenge it to open
battle and withdrew in early December. In August 1184 Saladin
again attacked Kerak, setting up no less than nine catapults which
so harassed the garrison that, in the words of a Muslim observer,
'No Frank can put his head out without receiving an arrow in the
eye...nothing remains but to fill in the fosse [ditch].'[3] But the
army of Jerusalem crossed the Jordan to the north of the Dead
Sea, and Saladin moved towards them. Apparently neither side
was seeking a battle, and though the Muslims mounted raids in
the north towards Nablus and Jenin, no serious action ensued.

The two sieges of Kerak, however, demonstrate a new military
reality. By the mid-twelfth century the settlers in the kingdom of
Jerusalem had come to realize that the relatively simple fortifications upon which they had hitherto relied were no longer powerful enough. Belvoir, built in 1168–70 by the Hospitallers, was a
new kind of fortification in which the outer walls were supported
against attack by an inner castle. But this was not simply a
concentric castle because the walls were lined with strong
covered stone galleries which sheltered the defenders who could
fire from well-protected narrow loops rather than exposing
themselves on the tops of the walls. In this way the concentric

castle was immensely strengthened by a layered defence, as well as a deep and wide moat. Kerak, presumably because of its exposed position, was developed along these lines in the 1170s. Yet this was not enough because on the occasion of both sieges Muslim armies all but took Kerak in a few days; this reinforced the lesson of Jacob's Ford which had fallen quickly to a determined attack. In 1184 the tower of Jenin, in which the population had sought refuge, was quickly destroyed by a Muslim raid. The military leaders of Jerusalem could hardly miss the significance of this—all fortifications were vulnerable and more dependent than ever on the field army to relieve them from Muslim attack.

That Saladin did not successfully conclude his sieges at Kerak in 1183 or 1184 probably reflected his caution. Montgisart in 1177 had taught him that confronting the Christian army on its own ground was dangerous. He was probably looking for a cheap success at Kerak which would redound to his glory, but not to take serious risks as he had in the earlier campaigns in the Galilee. He had other fish to fry, and most notably he needed to settle with his Muslim enemies and especially the Zengids of Mosul. This undoubtedly prompted him to make a truce with Jerusalem in 1185. The kingdom was eager to oblige him because Baldwin IV had died in March 1185, and thereafter the land was afflicted by drought. In this difficult situation the barons of Jerusalem advised Count Raymond to make truces with Saladin.

The truce with Jerusalem was to include Tripoli and Antioch, and to last for four years. At the same time Saladin arranged a peace with the Byzantine empire and with the Armenians in Cilicia which covered their relations with the sultan of Iconium with whom Saladin also wanted to establish good relations. This intense diplomatic activity enabled Saladin to march with a great army into the Jazira whose princes he reduced to obedience. Although he fell seriously ill during this campaign of 1186 Saladin now commanded a great empire over Jazira, Syria, and Egypt, though in much of it his power could only be exercised through intermediary lords and everything, therefore, depended on his personal prestige. He was also under pressure, because after a period of intense warfare against Muslim rivals he needed to do something about the holy war against the infidels which he had so loudly and often proclaimed. As he turned his mind in that direction, developments within the kingdom of Jerusalem could only give him encouragement.

Our knowledge of the very dramatic events which culminated in Hattin in the years 1185–7 depends on some rather curious sources. The great historian of the Latin East was William of Tyre, who wrote a history of the crusades and the Latin East from the beginnings until his death in 1184. About 1220 William's history was translated into Old French. The translation was then, probably at some point in the mid- to late 1230s, brought up to date by splicing on to the end post-1184 material from a work known as the *Chronicle of Ernoul and Bernard the Treasurer*.[4] This is a compilation dating from the early 1230s which incorporated material from a lost history by Ernoul, a squire of Balian of Ibelin who was one of the most prominent of the great barons of Jerusalem. Thus was created the first version of what are known as the *Old French Continuations of William of Tyre*. Ernoul's account of the events of 1185–7 is thus embedded in the texts of both the *Chronicle of Ernoul and Bernard the Treasurer* and the *Continuations*, although how far it was modified by later editors is hard to say. In the 1240s this first version of the *Continuations* was substantially expanded to form the account we know as the *Colbert-Fontainbleau Continuation*, and that in turn was developed *c*.1250 to produce the version known to us as the *Lyons Continuation*.[5] All three of these are recognizably similar, but there are also differences, and they all have gaps. Their variations are particularly notable in the story of the Battle of Hattin as we shall see. An entirely independent account of Hattin and the fall of the kingdom is to be found in the anonymous *De Expugnatione Terrae Sanctae Libellus* whose author tells us that he fought at the siege of Jerusalem when Saladin captured the city after Hattin.[6] All these works seems to have been altered and edited in the course of time, and it must be emphasized that *Ernoul* and the *Continuations* were written a very long time after the events they describe.[7]

In August 1186 Baldwin V died. This should have triggered the procedure agreed under Baldwin IV, but in fact what happened was a conspiracy and a coup. The child had been at Acre when he perished in the care of his guardian, Joscelin of Courtenay. We are told that Joscelin successfully persuaded Raymond of Tripoli not to proceed himself immediately to Jerusalem, but to permit Joscelin to take the body there for burial. Quite why this was thought desirable is not at all clear. Perhaps the argument was that it would avoid an unseemly clash of rival personalities during the funeral. Equally, however, Raymond may well have supposed that as *bailli* nothing could be done without his agreement, and so preferred to gather his friends and allies at Nablus, in the land of his close friend Baldwin of Ibelin, in anticipation of the political struggles which must inevitably ensue. In fact his enemies swiftly gathered at Jerusalem.

Despite all that had happened, Sybil now claimed to be the natural inheritor and she could count on powerful support from Gerard of Ridefort, master of the Hospital and a personal enemy of Raymond, together with Reynald of Châtillon, lord of Kerak, and Heraclius the patriarch. They proclaimed Sybil the true ruler of the kingdom and shut the gates of Jerusalem, fearful lest Raymond and his friends at Nablus attack the city. Sybil's allies, aware that Guy was disliked, insisted that she divorce him, and she seemed to agree to this. Before a coronation could be carried out, Sybil and her friends needed the crowns of Jerusalem which were kept in a safe with two keys, one held by the master of the Temple and the other by the master of the Hospital. Gerard of Ridefort was happy to use his, but Roger des Moulins, master of the Hospital, at first refused, perhaps wary of breaking the oath which he had sworn to respect the succession arrangements laid down by Baldwin IV. However, in the end he surrendered his key and Heraclius, as patriarch of Jerusalem, crowned Sybil as queen. Once consecrated, Sybil reaffirmed her marriage and proclaimed Guy king as her consort although this was deeply offensive to Raymond and the barons gathered at Nablus. When he was crowned his immediate followers shouted in triumph: 'Despite the *Polains*, we shall have a Poitevin as king.'[8]

The leaders of these *polains*, the second- and third-generation western inhabitants of the kingdom, were uncertain how to proceed. Raymond proposed that the barons assembled at Nablus should crown Isabel and Humphrey of Toron and advance on Jerusalem. But the couple fled and made submission to Guy and almost all the barons then decided that they had no option except to do homage to Guy, for as they said to Raymond: 'Sire, since it has come to pass that there is a king in Jerusalem, we cannot set up in opposition to him for this would only invite censure.'[9]

In reality, much as they disliked Guy, the barons had little alternative. Once crowned, Sybil's position was immensely strengthened, for consecration truly made a ruler. In 1066 even William of Normandy did not doubt that Harold, once consecrated, was actually a king. To undo what had been done posed real difficulties and would have involved a civil war from which most evidently shrank. Moreover, almost all of them probably had doubts about disinheriting Sybil in the way envisaged in 1183 by Baldwin IV, because it would have been an offence to the hereditary principle.

Raymond returned to Tiberias in his lands of the Galilee, while his strongest supporter, Baldwin of Ibelin, departed for Antioch leaving his lands to his brother, Balian. Guy took the homage of the remainder of the lords of the kingdom, but he could hardly have been unaware that they lacked any enthusiasm for his government. Gerard of Ridefort advised Guy to gather an army and to besiege Raymond in Tiberias. Gerard hated Raymond. It is said that he first came to the East as a mercenary, and, presumably because he was proficient, Raymond of Tripoli promised him a good marriage. When the lord of Botron in the county of Tripoli died, his daughter seemed a perfect match, but Raymond was apparently swayed by the offer of her weight in gold to give her hand to a rich Pisan merchant. Gerard regarded the merchant as no more than a mere common peasant, and was so enraged that he broke with Raymond and joined the Templars. He was elected as their master in 1184. At the moment that Guy was made king, Gerard is said to have cried, 'This crown is well worth the marriage of Botron.'[10]

In the face of this malice in high places Raymond turned to Saladin who sent troops to garrison Tiberias and offered every kind of support. In return Raymond promised to allow Muslim raiding parties access across his lands. At a time when Saladin's power was clearly on the increase and his threat to the kingdom gathering weight, this was truly a betrayal. However, many within the kingdom must have sympathized with Count Raymond, and Balian of Ibelin persuaded Guy to disperse his forces and to open negotiations with Raymond because any attack on Tiberias would risk provoking Saladin. Envoys were sent to Raymond who demanded the return of Beirut which had been granted him to defray his expenses as *bailli*, but that was held by Guy's great supporter, Joscelin of Courtenay. So the political deadlock continued.

Then, in late 1186 or early 1187, the crisis deepened. Reynald of Châtillon, in breach of the truce in force between Jerusalem and Saladin, seized a rich caravan passing between Cairo and Damascus. Saladin demanded restitution, and Guy, appalled by the likely consequences of this provocation, required Reynald to comply. But Reynald 'replied that he would not do so, for he was lord of his land, just as Guy was lord of his, and he had no truces with the Saracens'.[11] This was a novel doctrine of sovereignty, but its real force was that Guy dared not offend a powerful supporter. For Saladin, who was already gathering his forces, this was an excellent pretext for ending the peace with Jerusalem. He could call upon troops from his own lands of Egypt and Syria, but also, as a result of his recent successes, recruit forces from as far afield as the Jazira and Iraq. Throughout the months of April and May Saladin's men ruthlessly ravaged the lands of the lordship of Kerak without any response from the kingdom of Jerusalem. By March 1187 a huge Muslim army was starting to gather south of Damascus, though it was as yet unclear where Saladin would make his main effort. In addition, Saladin had taken pains to intimidate Antioch by demonstrations against its frontiers.

Beyond this he was careful to cultivate the new emperor of Byzantium, Isaac Angelus (1185–95), who had recently overthrown and killed Andronicus, and who was accordingly grateful for the recognition.

In the face of this grave danger Guy gathered the leading men of the kingdom. According to *Ernoul* all advised him to make peace with the count of Tripoli. On 29 March 1187 it was decided that a mission of conciliation should be sent to Count Raymond, led by the masters of the Temple and the Hospital, Joscius, archbishop of Tyre, Balian of Ibelin, and Reginald of Sidon. The delegation was broadly representative of the ruling circles in the kingdom of Jerusalem, containing as it did clerics and laymen, as well as friends and enemies of the count and some not perceived as having taken sides. This indicates a really serious attempt to reach a solution. Reginald did not travel with the others who went to Nablus where Balian left them to attend to his own affairs. The two masters and the archbishop of Tyre then moved on to La Fève (Afula), which they reached on 30 April, expecting Balian to join them there that evening. In the meantime Saladin had ordered his son, al-Afdal, who was close to the Sea of Galilee, to send a raid under the command of his trusted emir, Keukburri, into the kingdom across the lands of his ally, Raymond of Tripoli. Raymond had little alternative but to agree. He insisted, however, that the raiders must return within a day and avoid attacking any settlement, and sent careful warnings to all the nearby towns and villages. Clearly what Keukburri had in mind was to ravage the countryside and he was prepared to accept these limitations in the interests of good relations with Count Raymond. However, when the two masters heard about the Muslim force they decided to attack it.

It is hard not to see political considerations behind this decision. By shattering Keukburri's troops the two masters would put themselves and the king in a very strong position vis-à-vis Count Raymond. On 1 May 1187 they stripped nearby castles of their garrisons to raise a force of some eighty to ninety Templars led by James of Mailly, the marshall of the order, along with ten Hospitallers, and proceeded to Nazareth. There they were joined by forty royal knights who guarded the city. They encountered the Muslims, many of whom were watering their horses, at the springs of Cresson. It is said that their numbers, put by both Christian and Muslim sources at about 7,000, made James of Mailly hesitate until he was taunted by Gerard: 'You love your blond head too well to want to lose it!' So it happened that 140 knights, although massively outnumbered, charged into the enemy. The initial charge of the knights drove the Turks before them, but then they were engulfed and annihilated by superior numbers. This might have been the result of a deliberate ambush in which the smaller part of the Muslim force was sent ahead and feigned flight to draw the Latins into a trap. However, it may simply be that Gerard and his men happened to launch their attack just before the main enemy came into sight and that what followed was a chance encounter. The latter is more likely, because the Muslim sources make it clear that the battle was hard and far from a foregone conclusion. The forty knights from Nazareth surrendered, but almost all the members of the orders were killed including the master of the Hospital. Only Gerard and two other Templars escaped. To make matters worse, when he arrived at Nazareth Gerard of Ridefort had urged the citizens to come out in arms to help to collect the spoils of victory. These foot soldiers and their followers were cut down or enslaved by the victorious Muslims, while the squires of the killed or captured knights made their escape on horseback. This was a considerable triumph for Saladin, and the raiders returned past Tiberias brandishing the heads of the dead on spears and parading their prisoners.

Raymond of Tripoli, deeply shamed by his responsibility for the losses at Cresson, now expelled Saladin's troops from Tiberias, reconciled himself with Guy, and performed homage as a vassal for his lordship of Galilee. On the count's advice Guy appealed to Bohemond III of Antioch who sent fifty knights led by his son Raymond. Guy now made great efforts to raise an army large enough to face Saladin's host, and in doing this he stripped all the cities and castles of the kingdom of their garrisons. Gerard of Ridefort made a major contribution to this process. As part of his penance for the martyrdom of Archbishop Thomas Becket in 1173, King Henry II of England (1152–89) promised to go to Jerusalem. To cover his costs he deposited huge sums with the masters of the Temple and the Hospital. Gerard now spent this money raising troops. This was technically a misappropriation of funds, but given that Saladin was now gathering a huge invasion army, a perfectly reasonable one.

Immediately after his reconciliation with King Guy, Count Raymond returned to strengthen the fortifications of Tiberias. Once that was done he obeyed the king's order to gather his men at Saforie where the army of Jerusalem was to concentrate. Guy was raising the biggest army possible, and this took time. The main strike-force consisted of some 1,200 heavily armoured knights, of whom about 600 were provided by the orders. In addition, by offering generous wages, drawn from Henry II's money, something like 4,000 light cavalry and 15,000 foot came to Saforie. This was by far the greatest force ever raised by the kingdom of Jerusalem. But formidable as it was, King Guy seems to have had no plan for its use because, as we shall see, there was an open discussion at Acre and this continued until the eve of battle on 2 July 1187. This paralysis of will was the real consequence of the bitter conflicts within the kingdom for Guy was painfully aware that many disliked him, and so he was unable to impose a course of action. In 1183, aware that he did not have the confidence of the army, he had been equally indecisive. As a result, between early May and late June 1187 the kingdom was completely passive, conceding the initiative to Saladin.

By late May 1187 Saladin had mustered his forces on the Golan Heights where plentiful springs could supply his army with water, the single most important commodity for an army moving in high summer across a parched land. His army seems to have been enormous. At its heart were 12,000 regular cavalry, but they were supported by numerous other horsemen raised from across the vast lands where Saladin had influence, together with a mass of infantry including many *ghazi*, religious volunteers. It is possible that altogether some 40,000 men were mustering for the attack on Jerusalem. Saladin was confident after his recent successes and he encouraged his men with the memory of the Battle of Bador in 624 when, as the Koran recounts, Muhammad led his army to victory over the hostile Quraish of Mecca.

Gathering such a huge army and establishing lines of communication and supply took time. Moreover the Latins offered to discuss peace terms, and many of Saladin's chief men were prepared to consider them. As a result, it was not until 30 June that Saladin crossed the Jordan at Sinnabra and entered the kingdom of Jerusalem. His army ascended the mighty slope of the western side of the Jordan valley and established its main camp at Kafr Sabt. This place, with its plentiful springs, was on the edge of the high plateau which rises on the west to a ridge beyond which is the valley in which Saforie is situated. The northern edge is bordered by rocky outcrops, rising to the twin peaks of the Horns of Hattin which stand over a great depression in the land that extends eastwards to drop sharply to Tiberias and the Sea of Gaililee. In this way Saladin was allowed to dominate the roads to Tiberias and to establish himself securely within striking distance of that city. The great Muslim historian Ibn al-Athir is quite clear that the whole purpose of Saladin's expedition was to bring the enemy to battle: 'His purpose in besieging Tiberias had only been that the Franks should leave their position so that he could engage them.'[12] He was then able to carry out a careful reconnaissance of the whole area as a result of which he concluded that the plain around Hill 311 and the Horns of Hattin was suitable for a battle. The contrast with 1182 is striking: then the army of Jerusalem had marched across the plateau to threaten his attack on Baisan and they had not hesitated to challenge him using castles as a base.

As the royal army gathered, Guy moved to Acre where on 30 June news came of Saladin's threat to Tiberias. Guy then called a meeting of the chief barons which revealed a very deep divergence of opinion over how to react to this threat. Many, amongst them Gerard of Ridefort and Reynald of Châtillon, urged an immediate attack because the king 'was in the early days of his kingship, and if he let himself appear as a fool in the eyes of the Saracens, Saladin would take advantage of him, and thereafter he would not be able to hold out against him but would lose the kingdom'.

Given that the army now gathering was the biggest Jerusalem had ever fielded, this was not altogether bad advice and Guy must have remembered very vividly that it was failure to fight in 1183 that had led to his downfall. But others, led by Raymond of Tripoli, were against seeking battle. Count Raymond advised the king to ask for more aid from Antioch, to procure the return of Baldwin of Ibelin, and to strengthen all the fortifications of the kingdom, pointing out that even if Tiberias fell, the enemy army would eventually melt away. This was impressive, given that Tiberias was Raymond's city and that his wife Eschiva was trapped there and appealing for help. There was much to be said for this course of action also, because Saladin needed success to keep his army together: his men, tough professionals and others alike, were in the business of war for gain. The booty of Tiberias would hardly satisfy them and the problems of continuing the war against great cities of the kingdom of Jerusalem were immense. Twice before, in 1182 and 1183, Saladin had invaded and then run out of steam. On the other hand, Raymond was not disinterested in what he suggested, because the call for Baldwin of Ibelin to return would strengthen his political position. What is striking about this council was the bitterness. Count Raymond was accused to his face of bad faith by Gerard and Reynald of Châtillon who alleged that 'his counsel was not good and was "mingled with the hair of the wolf"'.[13]

Raymond's response to this was to demand that the army should go to the relief of Tiberias. This appears paradoxical since he was advising against this very course of action. However, the generally accepted practice of the kingdom was that the royal army should go to the aid of a threatened vassal (in this case Count Raymond's wife, Eschiva), so this was the default position if no other course of action was accepted. In fact, it is clear that no decision had been taken because the debate was resumed after the leaders moved to Saforie where the army was concentrating. The morale of the army was bolstered by the arrival of the 'True Cross' which had been discovered shortly after the crusader conquest of Jerusalem in 1099. It was often carried in the army by the Patriarch of Jerusalem, but on this occasion Heraclius preferred to dally with his mistress, Paschia de Riveri, known as the 'La Patriarchesse', and as a result this most holy of relics was carried into battle by the bishop of Acre, and when he was killed, the bishop of Ramla.

On 1 July Saladin himself appeared before Saforie, but his challenge for battle was ignored and he could hardly attack such a strong and well-watered position. There another council of the leaders was called. Interestingly the anonymous author of one of our sources, who is highly critical of the decision to seek battle, says that at first, 'All advised that at dawn they should march out, accompanied by the Lord's cross, ready to fight the enemy, with all the men armed and arrayed in battle formation.'[14]

This readiness in the army and amongst some of the leaders for a direct confrontation with a huge enemy force demands explanation for although the Latins may not have known exact numbers, they must have had some inkling of what they were up against. Presumably they knew something of its disparate nature and were fortified by knowledge of their own numbers. Count Raymond did not share this enthusiasm, and argued forcefully against precipitate action. He pointed out that if Saladin seized Tiberias and then still sought battle, the Jerusalemite army could concentrate near Acre. They could then choose when and where to give battle, secure in the knowledge that if they lost the contest they could easily take refuge behind powerful fortifications. On 2 July Saladin seized the city of Tiberias whose people fled into the citadel under the command of Countess Eschiva. That evening Guy called yet another council of war to consider what to do. After more acrid debate it was apparently agreed that Raymond's advice should be followed—the army would stay at Saforie and watch events. On the basis of this decision the leaders went to bed. Yet, in the morning, Guy issued orders to move eastwards. This was an astonishing reversal of policy, explained in our chronicles by a remarkable story. In the night after the decision to wait at Saforie was taken, Gerard of Ridefort had stayed behind with the king and advised him to give battle:

> Sire, do not trust the advice of the count for he is a traitor, and you well know that he has no love for you and wants you to be put to shame and lose the kingdom. I advise you to move off immediately together with the rest of us, and let us go and defeat Saladin. This is the first crisis that you have encountered since you became king. If you do not leave this camp Saladin will come to attack you, and if you withdraw at his attack the shame and reproach will be all the greater for you.[15]

The next morning the barons were amazed to be told to prepare to march out for battle and demanded to know how this decision had come about. But Guy was imperious: 'You have no right to ask me by whose counsel I am doing this. I want you to get on your horses and leave here and head towards Tiberias.'[16]

The quarrels which divided the leaders of the kingdom of Jerusalem at this critical junction have hypnotized all who have studied the subject, not least because the contemporaries and near-contemporaries, who wrote the sources on which our knowledge is based, placed so much emphasis on them as the cause of the disaster which followed. A young squire, Ernoul, who was almost certainly in the personal following of Balian of Ibelin, commented savagely that the king agreed with all that Gerard demanded because he 'did not dare contradict him, and so he did what he commanded, for he loved and feared him because he had made him King and because he had handed over the treasure of the King of England'.[17] Undoubtedly there was truth in this. After all, Raymond of Tripoli was advising Guy to do what he himself had savagely condemned Guy for doing in 1183, thus engineering his downfall. Guy must have felt that he was being set up by Raymond.

It is very evident that the military debate at Acre and Saforie was coloured by the bitter rivalries which had afflicted the kingdom for so many years, and by the general lack of confidence in Guy amongst many of the barons. There was a good case for both the courses of action which were advanced. Battle might destroy Saladin. Watching him closely and seizing opportunities might be wise. The trouble was that Saladin had been allowed so much time to establish himself west of the Jordan that the debate had resolved itself into a choice between staying either at Acre or at Saforie, thereby conceding the initiative to the enemy, or marching through a dry land to fight him at a place of his choosing. And underlying this was deep distrust of Guy's leadership by many in the army.

To understand the battle it is necessary to grasp the topography of the area. Saforie is about 26 kilometres west of Tiberias, and set on the southern side of an east–west valley, Bet Netofa (Arabic Buttauf which crusaders called 'Vallé Batof') along which passed the Roman road from Acre to Tiberias (approximately modern route 77). The valley is dominated on its northern side by

Mount Turan, at whose foot lies the village of Turan with its springs; this is only 14 kilometres from Tiberias. From Turan the road clings fairly closely to Mount Turan and rises gently towards the plateau, but the countryside around it remains open and suitable for mounted manoeuvre. The road forks about 1 kilometre east of Turan. The right branch turns southwards up to the plateau and, via Kafr Sabt, to the crossings of the Jordan at Sinnabra to the south of the Sea of Galilee. The other and more northerly branch climbs from Turan, at 200 metres above sea level, until about 3–4 kilometres east of Turan it was cut by a north–south route (approximately modern route 65). West of this road and north of the east–west road was the pool and spring of Maskana at 220 metres above sea level. Some 2 kilometres eastward the Roman road veered north around Hill 311 (now the site of Kibbutz Lavi), south of which was the hill now called el-Khirbeh. The plateau sloped steeply down to Saladin's camp at Kafr Sabt some 4 kilometres to the south-east. In effect the road north of Hill 311 enters a pass with the two hills to its south and the rocky edge of the great depression to the north. The rocky edge rises eastwards to what are called the 'Horns of Hattin', twin hills marking the site of an ancient volcano, below which and somewhat to the north are the springs of Kafr Hattin. On the Horns are the remains of a hill fort. Beyond the Horns, the road follows the edge of the depression to the end of the plateau where a branch leads north-east to Tiberias while the main route descends steeply to the Jordan crossings south of the Sea of Galilee.

On the morning of 3 July Guy and his army set off eastwards, probably via Mashhad. They turned north down onto the road to Tiberias, and advanced towards Turan. They were organized in three boxes. The vanguard was commanded by Raymond of

Tripoli, for it was the custom that the army should be led by the lord across whose lands they were fighting. The king, accompanied by the Holy Cross, commanded the central box, while Balian of Ibelin was in charge of the rearguard which was largely manned by the Templars and Hospitallers. Within each box were the mounted knights, the strike force of the army, and they were surrounded by infantry and archers whose task was to hold off the enemy horse-archers who would try to wound the all-important horses. As they debouched onto the Roman road to Tiberias this formation would have extended over a considerable distance. The road was about 10 metres wide, which means that the knights could have advanced along it in a column six wide. It seems likely that each block of knights numbered about 400, so that allowing 3 metres for each horse, the heavy cavalry in any one box would have occupied about 200 metres of road. In addition the army also had a large number of light horse, turcopoles, who probably kept close to the knights. We know that the army had a substantial amount of baggage because towards the end of the battle they tried to set up tents to block enemy charges. We are not told if this paraphernalia was carried on wagons or pack animals, but we can assume they covered at least an additional 60 metres of road. In addition a contemporary Muslim letter reports that after the battle many women and children were captured, so presumably there were non-combatants as well. Around this core were the infantry and archers, forming a perimeter at least 10 metres outside and all around the knights and the baggage. Thus any one of these boxes would have extended over some 400 metres or more of road. Since the boxes would have been somewhat separated, the army would have been spread out over more than 1 kilometre of road, rolling like a battering ram towards the enemy. In the heat and dust of this movement communication between the three commanders would have been enormously difficult.

The march from Saforie was immediately contested by the Muslim army, but probably only lightly because Saladin was busy in the vicinity of Tiberias. He only arrived at the edge of the plateau towards noon when Guy's army was approaching Turan. This movement significantly changed the balance of advantage between the two armies because Guy was now only about 14–15 kilometres from Tiberias and only 10 kilometres from Saladin's main camp at Kafr Sabt. As Saladin looked down on the enemy he must have been deeply worried lest they establish themselves at Turan. In a letter to Baghdad written shortly after the battle Saladin spoke of 'the hawks of the Frankish infantry and the eagles of their cavalry hovering around the water'. But, he went on, 'Satan incited Guy to do what ran counter to his purpose', that is to say he left Turan and mounted the climb to the plateau. This was, indeed, the crucial decision which led to defeat. It seems that the Jerusalemite army hesitated at Turan. The spring there now yields very little water, but Saladin's obvious concern—and relief—as the enemy left Turan suggests that in 1187 it was much more abundant. Certainly, if there was enough water, at Turan Guy would have been in an unassailable position very like that at Saforie, and from there he could threaten to advance and oblige Saladin to keep his forces on the edge of the plateau in readiness. This was a game which Saladin's army could not play indefinitely because it was profitless in every sense. However Guy did not stop at Turan. Certainly if his army could reach the plateau in good order they would be in a menacing position. Ibn al-Athir, who was a member of Saladin's intimate circle, clearly believed their purpose was to attack Saladin's camp: 'The Muslims had camped where there was a spring, it being high summer and extremely hot. The Franks experienced thirst and were unable to reach that spring because of the Muslims, who had destroyed what cistern water there was.'[18] Guy may also have had the thought that if there were difficulties, Turan could be a place of refuge to which they could return.

Guy now plunged his army into a situation where Saladin could wear down his army and choose the place of battle. For numbers immediately began to tell. When he assembled his army Saladin had divided it into units of manoeuvre under trusted lieutenants. The right wing, traditionally the offensive element, went to his ambitious and able nephew Taqi al-Din, while the left was given to a renowned warrior, Muzaffar al-Din, called Gok-bori, the 'Blue Wolf'. Saladin controlled the middle unit. The large forces under Taqi al-Din and Gokbori were now dispatched to seize Turan and to harass the advancing Latin army on its southern flank. At the same time Saladin kept ample forces on the edge of the plateau so that the Jerusalemites dared not deploy and turn to charge those who were harassing them. The Muslims mercilessly pressed their attacks upon the crusader columns, and most particularly concentrated on the rearguard manned by the Templars under the command of Balian of Ibelin. These thrusts were made the more effective because the Franks had no water.

The army of Jerusalem certainly had a supply train with them, but it was impossible to carry much water because of its weight and that of the necessary containers. During the Vietnam War American infantry operating in the jungle heat generally found it necessary to carry about 5 litres of water per man. Humidity, of course, was not a problem on the road to Hattin as it was in

Vietnam, but the temperatures would have been very high—perhaps around 90 °F. Soldiers would have been able to carry water skins, but their content would be limited by weight. The most important effect of the heat and lack of water would have been to exhaust the horses, and particularly the heavily laden warhorses of the knights and lords who formed their strike force. A 1,000-lb horse needs over 45 litres per day, though much of this is normally taken in the form of lush fodder. In adverse conditions of heat and humidity a horse can lose up to 20 litres of water per hour, especially if, as on this day, it is not able to graze on green moist grass. The summer heat and lack of water and pasturage would have badly weakened all the animals. As they reached the general area of Maskana it became evident that, although they had actually come only about 4–5 kilometres, the army was in crisis. One medieval western chronicler of the event remarked: 'The Turks kept engaging them and so impeded their progress. The heat was very great and that was a source of great affliction, and in that valley there was nowhere they could find water.'[19] And another, who provides a generally convincing account, says bluntly: 'At this place they were so constrained by enemy attacks and by thirst that they wished to go no further.'[20] At the head of the column, as the army approached the top of the slope, Count Raymond would have been able to see that Saladin's main force was deployed across the two hills to the south, and that his army would have to force a passage through the narrow gap north of Hill 311. Our sources all agree that the army halted, but they disagree as to how this came about, and even as to where they actually stopped for the night.

The anonymous author of *De Expugnatione Terrae Sanctae Libellus* was probably not present but he seems to have been writing very shortly after and according to him Raymond sent a message to Guy urging the need to press on through the gap north of Hill 311: 'We must hurry and pass through this area, so that we and our men may be safe near the water. Otherwise we will be in danger of making camp at a waterless spot.' At first Guy agreed that 'We will pass through at once'. However, the enemy stepped up the attacks on the rearguard, and, apparently under the influence of this, Guy changed his mind and ordered that tents be pitched, leading Count Raymond to cry: 'Alas, Lord God, the battle is over! We have been betrayed unto death. The Kingdom is finished!'[21] The accounts in the *Continuations* and *Ernoul* say that Count Raymond himself suggested to the king that they should make camp and Guy 'gladly accepted this bad advice, though when he gave him good advice he would never take it'.[22]

Such differences between stories reflect the attitudes of their writers to Raymond and to the whole question of blame for Hattin and greatly complicate the business of understanding the battle. However, all the sources see this as a key decision and some report that there was opinion in favour of an immediate attack: 'Some people in the host said that if the Christians had pressed on to meet the Saracens, Saladin would have been defeated.'[23] How realistic this was depends considerably on where the army was by this time. The *Ernoul* says that they were halfway between Saforie and Tiberias, while the *Lyons Continuation* suggests no location. The *Colbert-Fontainbleau Continuation* says clearly that the army was on one of the Horns of Hattin: 'at the summit of the mountain at the place called the Horns of Hattin'.[24] By contrast, the author of *De Expugnatione Terrae Sanctae Libellus* reports that they actually stopped at Maskana and this is borne out by other references to the place.[25] Now Maskana was a very small place with a minor spring and pool which was inadequate to supply the army, so it seems unlikely that our anonymous author would have made this up. Moreover, on the next day all the accounts make clear that the army got close to the gorge between the two Horns of Hattin because some of the knights escaped down it. If they had been on the western Horn (the nearest to Maskana) they would not have needed to fight their way to reach it, and if the Horn referred to was actually the eastern one, they would have been safely in possession of the entry to the gorge. All this suggests strongly that the camp site was around Maskana and that the *De Expugnatione Terrae Sanctae Libellus* is to be believed on this point.

In fact on the next day, 4 July, King Guy's army must have managed to march across the highest point on the battlefield, the watershed, which extends south to north over Hill 311 roughly north-north-east (towards Mount Nimrin) to somewhere within striking distance of the Hattin gorge. It is at least possible that if they had continued on 3 July they could have reached the lower slopes of the western Horn. There they would have been significantly closer to Tiberias than at Maskana, and they could have commanded the gorge between the Horns which leads gently down to the springs at Hattin. Further, they could have threatened Saladin's camp at Kafr Sabt. But the main consequence of this decision to halt at Maskana was that the army would still have to fight and under adverse circumstances after a night which would bring no water and no rest.

Saladin had handled the conflict on 3 July with ability and purpose. He greatly feared a concerted charge by the enemy which, if well timed and directed, had the potential to destroy his army. This is why he had refused to meet Guy in the plain by Turan. It is also why he had harassed the enemy column as it ascended to Maskana, but kept his main force aloof so that it was not exposed to a devastating attack. At the very forefront of his mind would have been the fear that any initial setback might cause his composite army to break up and melt away. This cautious and sensible outlook continued to serve him well.

Saladin understood the importance of water. During the night of 3/4 July he surrounded the army of Jerusalem. Into the mountainous and broken rocky ground to the north he sent his infantry, effectively blocking any possibility of escape northwards from Maskana. His forces encircled their enemies so closely that one of them commented: 'if there had been a cat fleeing from the host of the Christians, it would have been unable to escape without the Saracens taking it'.[26]

During the night the Muslim infantry lit fires so that choking clouds of smoke drifted across the Christian camp intensifying the misery of thirst. The Muslim left wing under Gokbori prevented any retreat towards Turan, while Saladin's centre division strung across the hill of Lubieh stood to the south and Taqi al-Din's cavalry were athwart the road in front of the Christian army. On the morning of 4 July Saladin instructed that more fires be lit, presumably to take account of changes in wind direction. He also brought up ample water supplies on camels and had it poured away in the sight of the parched enemy. But Saladin still feared the might of a heavy cavalry charge, for he ordered that his army stand off until the heat of the day had further weakened the horses of the knights and increased the thirst of their men. According to one account five of Raymond of Tripoli's knights at this point deserted to Saladin and, by revealing the dire straits of the army, triggered him into ordering an advance.

What, at this point, were the Christians trying to do? We are very badly informed because no clear picture emerges from any of the western sources which, in any case, show little taste for recounting the detail of a horrific defeat. The Muslim sources focus on the doings of their own side. Guy apparently took counsel with Reynald of Châtillon and the master of the Temple who urged him to give battle. One interesting account reports that a knight John, who had often served in Turkish armies, advised that the best strategy was to launch a concerted mass charge at Saladin and the troops around him, because seizing or killing him would guarantee victory. The king then ordered his brother Amalric, constable of the kingdom, to organize the divisions, and 'He did as best he could'.[27] There is no real indication of what Amalric did, except that we know Count Raymond remained in the van, so it seems likely that, at least initially, they set off in the three successive boxes in which they had fought the day before.

Their goal, however, remains unclear. The main gambit of the westerners was to deliver a massive charge at the critical mass of the enemy army, but any such concentration of force as suggested by the knight John was now extraordinarily difficult, because to throw the knights at one of the main divisions of Saladin's forces, any one of which outnumbered them, would expose them to attack in the rear from the others. It seems likely that their main intention was to find water, and the nearest source was at the village of Hattin, some 5 kilometres to the north, but this was only accessible via the relatively gentle ravine which slopes down between the Horns of Hattin. This was about 2 kilometres ahead, and the way was blocked by Taqi al-Din's forces—and in any case Saladin had earlier established some infantry at the springs of Hattin. The Muslim sources clearly say that the enemy were headed towards the Lake of Tiberias, and forcing a way through and down the Hattin gorge was the obvious way to achieve that.

The sequence of events which followed is confused because our sources are so brief and unhelpful. The *Lyons Continuation* reports that Guy sent Count Raymond in a charge against the enemy, though it failed and only a few escaped, amongst them the count himself. After that there was heavy fighting 'between the hours of terce and nones' (9 a.m. to 3 p.m.) when there was a total collapse.[28] *Colbert-Fontainbleau* agrees with this sequence, but adds a highly significant detail—that the infantry or at least a significant group of them, deserted and it was only then that Guy unleashed Raymond's failed charge after which there was a total collapse.[29] This mass desertion by the infantry of Guy's army is recorded by the *Ernoul* which reports that 'The sergeants on foot went to give themselves up to the Saracens, their throats parched for distress of thirst'.[30] The anonymous author of *De Expugnatione Terrae Sanctae Libellus* amplifies this by saying that the infantry took flight 'to the very summit of a high mountain' and when the king and others begged them to come down, they refused, saying: 'We are not coming because we are dying of thirst and we will not fight.'[31] Without infantry to cover them Guy's cavalry were trapped between the mass of Saladin's mounted men all around to the south, and the Muslim infantry who could now occupy the rocky outcrops of the Horns. This is the force of the comment written by a Templar survivor of the battle in a very hasty letter to Europe that the enemy 'pressed upon us in some very bad rocks' and this is confirmed by other accounts.[32]

It seems certain that Raymond of Tripoli charged into the forces of Taqi al-Din. *Ernoul* and both the *Continuations* say that this was on the orders of King Guy, and that the enemy first opened their ranks, then closed upon them, killing all but twelve, amongst whom was Raymond himself. He seems to have broken through down the gorge between the Horns of Hattin into the plain, then turned north for Tyre. This is partially supported by the Muslim account of Ibn al-Athir according to whom,

> When he [Taqi al-Din] saw the Franks charge in such a desperate fashion, he knew that there was no possibility of standing firm to face them, so he ordered his men to make a path for them by which they could leave the field. This they did and the Count and his men rode away. The ranks were then closed again.[33]

The Anonymous *De Expugnatione Terrae Sanctae Libellus*, however, paints a different and very convincing portrait of an army confused and broken into pieces. He alone tells us that the rearguard, largely manned by the Templars, the Hospitallers, and the turcopoles, at some stage attempted a charge but on its failure were driven into the king's central battle. With his forces hopelessly disordered, Guy instructed that tents be put up on the lower slopes of the Horn to break up the enemy's charges. To add to the confusion Muslim infantry drove the leaderless and dispirited Jerusalemite foot off the top of the mountain back down into the battle. As a result of all this Count Raymond's division was cut off from the rest:

> They saw that there was a multitude of barbarians between themselves and the King, so that they could not get through.... They cried

out: 'Those who can get through may go, since the battle is not going in our favour'...A large group of pagans charged on our infantry and pitched them from the top of the steep mountain [the western Horn of Hattin] to whose summit they had previously fled. They destroyed the rest, taking some captive and killing others...Upon seeing this the Count and his men, who had been riding onward, together with Balian of Naples, Reginald of Sidon and other half-castes [*polains*], turned back. The speed of their horses in this confined space trampled down the Christians and made a kind of bridge, giving the riders a level path. In this manner they got out of that narrow place by fleeing over their own men, over the Turks and over the Cross. Thus it was that they escaped with only their lives.[34]

This is a vivid picture of the disintegration of the Jerusalemite army, and the terrible carnage which accompanied it, with the two sides badly mixed up and some knights riding down their own men in their haste to escape. It is interesting that the author of this work says it was the *polains* who got away. Perhaps, when the going got really rough, they abandoned Guy, for whom most had no time at all, for in the end he seems to have fought accompanied only by members of the orders and his own intimate followers including the Poitevins, who had earlier been so contemptuous of the *polains*.

This collapse seems to have happened as the army reached the eastern foot of the western Horn, moving towards the gorge which led down to the springs of Hattin. But the battle did not end then. Guy seems to have rallied all that remained of his cavalry around the 'True Cross' up on the slope of the western Horn of Hattin and from there made several charges 'which almost drove the Muslims from their positions, despite their numbers, had it not been for God's grace. However, the Franks did not charge and retire without suffering losses and they were gravely weakened by that.'[35] According to Saladin's son, al-Afdal:

> I was alongside my father during this battle. When the king of the Franks was on the hill with that band, they made a formidable charge against the Muslims facing them, so that they drove them back to my father...I looked towards him and he was overcome with grief and his complexion pale. He took hold of his beard and advanced, crying out 'Give the lie to the Devil'. The Muslims rallied, returned to the fight and climbed the hill....But the Franks rallied and charged again like the first time and drove the Muslims back to my father. He acted as he had on the first occasion and the Muslims turned upon the Franks and drove them back to the hill.[36]

After this Guy seems to have dismounted in an effort to use the tents and the ancient fortifications on the western Horn to defend the remains of his army, some 150 strong, but ultimately they were exhausted and dehydrated, so that, according to a Muslim chronicler, 'when they found no way of escape, they dismounted and sat on the ground'.[37]

Saladin had won an overwhelming victory. The army of Jerusalem had been totally destroyed, and the cities of the kingdom which had been stripped of their garrisons to fill its ranks lay at his mercy. King Guy must carry a heavy responsibility for this disaster, for he had allowed Saladin to establish himself unchallenged in a strong position close to Tiberias. He was clearly uncertain how to proceed once his army had gathered, and in the end pitched it into battle in the most unfavourable of circumstances, above all without water. Once battle was joined he failed to control events. This was a commander who failed at all levels. It is hard to dissent from the judgement of one of his subjects:

But the saying of Wisdom: 'Woe to the land whose King is a child and whose citizens dine in the morning'[38] was fulfilled in them. For our young King followed youthful counsel, while our citizens, in hatred and jealousy, ate their neighbors' meat. They departed from the advice which would have saved them and others. Because of their foolishness and simple-mindedness they lost land, people and selves.[39]

But Saladin handled his army exceptionally well, and in particular never granted the enemy an opportunity to launch a great charge. This was generalship of a very high order and it reaped the richest of rewards for the army of Jerusalem was totally destroyed. In the words of Ibn al-Athir, 'seeing the slain, you would not imagine that anyone had been taken alive, while seeing the captives, you would think that none could have been killed'.[40]

# 4

# Hattin

*Bloody Consequences*

I n the wake of the battle, Hattin seemed a decisive victory that opened endless possibilities. Little wonder that Saladin boasted:

> As soon as Allah the most high enables me to wrest the rest of the maritime plain, I plan to divide my realm among my aides, give them instructions, bid them farewell and cross the seas, pursuing the enemy to their island. There I shall destroy the last on the surface of the earth of those who do not believe in Allah.[1]

In the immediate aftermath of the battle his victorious army set about enjoying the fruits of victory. For most of the ordinary soldiers this meant taking prisoners who could be sold as slaves. This was the normal fate of defeated infantry who were not butchered or could not afford to pay ransoms for their release. So numerous were they that prices in the slave market at nearby Damascus are said to have collapsed, and a contemporary report claims that 'The Christian captives were so numerous that one was sold for a pair of sandals'.[2] Of the 1,200 knights and nobles in the Jerusalemite army, only some 200 seem to have escaped from the battlefield. The most important of these was Raymond of

Tripoli who fled to Tyre and then on to Tripoli where he died in September. Balian, lord of Ibelin, who had commanded the rear-guard of the army, also escaped, as did Reginald of Sidon and Joscelin of Courtenay. Other noble survivors had been able to surrender because their captors anticipated rich ransoms for their freedom. Perhaps in the process many had deserted Guy in his last stand on the slopes of Hattin.

The greatest captives of all, King Guy and Reynald of Châtillon, were brought before Saladin. He had twice vowed to kill Reynald, first because of his attacks on the Muslim Holy Places and again after his seizure of the caravan which had precipitated the war. Now Reynald was offered conversion to Islam as the only way of saving his life, and when he refused Saladin personally executed him. To us Reynald is an unattractive figure, arrogant, aggressive, and overbearing with something of the fanatic about him. But to contemporary western Christians he was a true champion of Christianity, 'The Elephant of Christ' who was commemorated as a martyr. The execution of Reynald terrified Guy, but Saladin reassured him: 'It has not been customary for princes to kill princes, but this man transgressed his limits, so he has suffered what he has suffered.'[3]

Many members of the military orders of the Hospital and Temple had been captured, and after the battle on 5 July Saladin ordered their execution. Their captors resisted, which is not surprising given the profit to be made from ransom, so Saladin was obliged to buy them:

> Therefore for every prisoner in these two categories Saladin offered fifty Egyptian dinars. Immediately 200 prisoners were brought to him and he ordered their heads to be struck off. He singled these out for

execution because they were the fiercest fighters of all the Franks. He wished to rid the Muslims of their wickedness.[4]

One of the very few Templars to escape, Terricus, immediately wrote to the pope to inform him of the disaster and remarked: 'In truth we believe on that day 230 of our brothers were beheaded, not counting the 60 who were killed on the first of May [the battle at the springs of Cresson].'[5] We can assume that the Hospital suffered comparable losses.

But, as Saladin quickly realized, the fact was that he had won a victory, but not the war. The kingdom of Jerusalem lay at his mercy, but he knew that Hattin was likely to provoke a response from Europe, so if he was to win the war it was essential for him to secure all the fortresses and cities, and above all the port cities of the Palestinian coast, thereby denying to the westerners bases from which a seaborne crusading army could attempt to recover all that was lost. The cities and castles of the kingdom had been stripped of their garrisons in order to produce the huge army which he had just destroyed, but he was perfectly well aware that a desperate population might hold out for quite a while behind strong walls. His army was certainly strong enough to take any of the cities and castles of the kingdom, but it would take time to capture all of them during which his men might grow tired, or help might arrive from Europe. Accordingly, Saladin resolved to offer generous terms in return for surrender, and more particularly to offer every consideration to the defeated leaders of the kingdom who could influence all others. Saladin seems to have been a man with remarkable humanitarian instincts, but it was this policy that laid the foundation for his later reputation for courtesy and kindness.

As a first step in this intelligent political and military strategy he received the capitulation of the citadel of Tiberias, and permitted Countess Eschiva to depart freely with her household. On 9 July he arrived before the great port of Acre. Its governor, Joscelin of Courtenay, seneschal of the kingdom was a great magnate, closely associated with King Guy. He had escaped from Hattin, but now immediately offered to capitulate on terms. The good sense of Saladin's generosity was immediately apparent because

> When the rest of the people heard that Count Joscelin had surrendered the city and had sent the keys to the Saracens, they were all furious and there was almost a major battle between them in the city. They said they would rather burn the town than surrender it to the Saracens, and some people actually started fires in the city.[6]

Saladin then intervened to reassure the citizens, who finally agreed to put out the fires and to accept the terms of capitulation which allowed them to go or stay, as they pleased. At the same time, detachments of Saladin's army accepted the surrender of Nablus, Haifa, Caeserea, Saffuriya, and Nazareth which had virtually no troops in them. By contrast, Jaffa, which held out against Saladin's brother, and Tibnin castle which resisted him, were stormed and their inhabitants sold into slavery. When Saladin's army approached Tyre, Reginald of Sidon, another close associate of Guy who had survived Hattin, was ready to come to terms. In the customary symbol of surrender he placed Saladin's banner upon the walls of the city.

But on 14 July Conrad of Montferrat, a man with a formidable military reputation, had arrived. He was a member of a famous north Italian house, whose elder brother, William, had married Sybil of Jerusalem and was the father of Baldwin V. Their father,

William V of Montferrat, was present at the coronation of Guy and was captured at Hattin. Conrad had sought his fortune at the court of the emperor Isaac Angelus in Constantinople where he helped put down a major rebellion, but in 1187 he intended to join his father in the Holy Land. His ship went first to Acre, only to be told that it was in Muslim hands—after which he diverted to Tyre. The city was well fortified and most of the survivors of Hattin had concentrated there; under Conrad's firm leadership they rejected surrender and cast down Saladin's standards from the city wall. Saladin withdrew and seized Sidon which Reginald surrendered to him. Saladin then turned south with his army and arrived before the strongly fortified city of Ascalon on 23 August. He brought with him King Guy to whom he promised freedom if he persuaded the city to capitulate. But Guy's exhortations, even when backed up by Gerard of Ridefort, were greeted with derision by the citizens. The siege was pressed at the cost of some notable Muslim casualties, but on 4 September it capitulated; its people were allowed to depart under escort to Egypt and subsequently embarked from Alexandria on western ships.

Saladin now turned his attention to Jerusalem which was packed full of refugees from the countryside around. He summoned representatives of the citizens to Ascalon, and when they refused immediate submission he made them an extraordinarily generous offer. The citizens were to be allowed to stay in the city and to enjoy freedom of movement within 8 kilometres of its walls, and would be supplied with food provided they swore to capitulate if no relief had arrived by Pentecost 1188. Arrangements of this kind, by which a besieged place promised submission if no relief arrived within a specified period—usually forty days—were common in Europe and not unheard of in the East, but in warfare between the religions this was unprecedented. Even so:

> They replied that if it pleased God they would never surrender the city where God had shed His blood for them to Saracens under such terms. When Saladin saw and heard their answer he swore he could never accept Jerusalem by treaty but instead would take it by force.[7]

The spirit shown by the ordinary city and country people of the Latin kingdom has been insufficiently remarked by historians. Their defiance at Acre, Ascalon, and Jerusalem stands in contrast to the supine surrenders offered by their leaders.

And indeed the leaders of the kingdom continued to pursue their own interests. On 20 September Saladin encamped beneath the walls of Jerusalem. Balian of Ibelin and his kinsman Hugh of Jubail, who had escaped from Hattin, begged Saladin to permit Hugh's son, Guillemin and Thomassin, Balian's nephew, to leave the city—and Saladin agreed. He had every reason to do so. Like Eschiva, the lady of Tiberias, these children were of no military value, and by being merciful he drew the old elite of Jerusalem further into his web of capitulation. The experience of popular resistance at Acre and Ascalon and the defiance of Jerusalem was a sobering one and Saladin must have been anxious to prevent any repetition.

But Balian had another request for Saladin. The Byzantine princess Maria Comnena had come to the Holy Land as the wife of King Amalric of Jerusalem. After her husband's death she married Balian. He knew that she was in Jerusalem and he asked to be allowed to enter the city and to escort her to the coast. Saladin had a very special reason for being accommodating to

Balian. Maria was the grand-niece of the former emperor Manuel I, and therefore belonged to the highest levels of Byzantine society. Saladin did not want needlessly to provoke the emperor Isaac Angelus by mistreating such a grand lady, particularly as Isaac might be persuaded to obstruct western attempts to aid the Holy Land. When Balian entered the city the patriarch Heraclius and the citizens begged him to stay because Jerusalem was in a poor condition to resist Saladin's great army. The city was full of refugees, and while they were determined, they lacked leadership for there were only two knights in the place:

> And I tell you in truth that the city was already so full of people, women and children who had taken refuge in the city when they heard it said that the king was captured and the Christians defeated; and I tell you well in truth that there were so many refugees that they could not be put in houses but had to camp in the middle of the streets.[8]

In the end Balian agreed to stay, but Saladin still permitted Maria Comnena to leave in safety. Balian conducted a vigorous resistance, and began by knighting sixty of the sons of the citizens in order to provide leadership. He and the patriarch Heraclius stripped the Holy Sepulchre of its silver covering in order to pay them and the other soldiers.

Despite the lack of troops, the citizens put up a brave fight. Saladin's army had approached the north-western corner of the city, and it would seem that some of the citizens sallied out to ensure that the enemy could not set up catapults within range of the walls. At the north-western corner of Jerusalem the walls stand at the top of a steep slope and this was undoubtedly important in the repulse of the enemy. On 25 September Saladin moved his troops around to the north-eastern corner of the city. When the people of Jerusalem saw his tents being struck they thought for a moment that he was giving up the siege after their staunch resistance, but it was an illusion. In fact the Muslim army established itself precisely where the crusaders had broken into Jerusalem in 1099, at a point where the lie of the land favours the attacker and the walls are, therefore, vulnerable. Saladin's army set up catapults and poured arrows upon the ramparts. The fighting which ensued was fierce. We are fortunate to have the account of an anonymous soldier who took part and later recorded his experiences in his *De Expugnatione Terrae Sanctae*:

> Arrows fell like raindrops, so that one could not show a finger above the ramparts without being hit. There were so many wounded that all the hospitals and physicians in the city were hard put to it just to extract the missiles from their bodies. I myself was wounded in the face by an arrow which struck the bridge of my nose. The wooden shaft has been taken out, but the metal tip has remained there to this day.[9]

By 29 September the Muslim sappers had created a breach in the wall and some of Saladin's soldiers occupied this north-eastern corner of the city. The defenders then attempted a sally 'through the gate which leads to Jehosephat',[10] presumably what is now called the Lion Gate, but they were driven back by the strong cavalry forces which Saladin kept close to his attackers for just this purpose. Thereafter morale amongst the defenders plummeted, and even large sums of money offered by the patriarch could not persuade men to fight. The fact was that the garrison, such as it was, was hopelessly outnumbered. They sent to ask Saladin for terms, and at first he refused, preferring to bathe the city in Christian blood. However, Balian was able to play a weak hand well, threatening that if the citizens faced massacre they would destroy everything within the walls, especially the Muslim shrines on the Temple Mount. This was no empty threat. Many in the city, including the author of *De Expugnatione* who certainly did not belong to the ruling class, felt a profound sense of shame at this surrender:

> Who could ever think that such a wicked thing would be done by Christians? To surrender of their own free will the tomb of Christ's resurrection, the noble Temple, the most sacred Mount Sion and the other places of the sacred city into the hands of unbelievers? O, the pain of it! There is no pain like this pain of ours![11]

The poor and many of the refugees feared, with every justification, that if the price of ransom was beyond them they would be sold into slavery.

There is no doubt that the position of the city was hopeless, but Saladin too was under pressure. Conrad of Montferrat was organizing resistance at Tyre and a Sicilian fleet was coming to the aid of the Christians. Saladin had to liberate Jerusalem because of its religious importance, but he knew that it had no strategic significance and that the efforts of Conrad and others were merely tokens of what was to come. In addition, a number of the kingdom's fortresses were still holding out against his troops, notably Kerak and Shawbak in Prince Reynald's fief of Outre-Jourdain, Hospitaller Belvoir, and Templar Safed to the north. To storm Jerusalem would cost blood and time, and also compromise Saladin's reputation for mercy which he had been at pains to cultivate as an instrument of policy. As a result he and Balian began a long process of haggling. Initially Saladin demanded

100,000 dinars as the ransom of the entire population, but Balian persuaded him that this was an impossible sum and in the end a tariff was worked out by which every adult male would pay 10 dinars, every woman 5, and every child 1: all who could make the payment would be free to leave with such of their possessions as they could carry and some were even allowed to keep their arms to protect the rest. The trouble was that many of the poor and of the refugees could not afford even this, but the Hospital was persuaded to part with the remainder of Henry II of England's money towards their ransom, and this, together with other contributions, was enough to free another 7,000: 'but the Templars and the Hospitallers did not give as much as they should, since, thanks to Saladin's assurances, they were not afraid that what they had would be seized by force'.[12]

An elaborate system was set up to ensure the probity of the transaction, and in the event Saladin and his brother, Saif al-Din, actually freed about 4,000 more of the captives. Even so it is believed that 11,000 were enslaved. Some women, presumably of the upper class, who had lost spouses at Hattin, approached Saladin and asked for his mercy, and he ordered the liberation of such of their husbands as he held. All those leaving Jerusalem were organized into three groups: the first with the Templars, the second with the Hospitallers, and the third under Balian and Heraclius. It was almost a caricature of the formation at Hattin. In the event their progress to the coast was fairly easy until they reached Christian territory where

> Reynald, who was the lord of Nephin, stationed his sergeants in a defile with orders to rob and despoil the people of Jerusalem as much as they could. So they seized what little Saladin had let the Jerusalemites keep...the count [Raymond of Tripoli] ordered the gates to be

shut against them so that none might enter, and he sent his men to
the defile that is called St William. There they seized the burgesses of
Jerusalem, and they robbed them and handled them so foully that it
would be shameful to tell of it. The people of Nephin and Tripoli
treated them worse than the Saracens.[13]

Saladin entered Jerusalem on 9 October, and almost his first act
was to topple the cross from the golden Dome of the Rock and
replace it with a Muslim crescent. He then returned to Damascus
where he collected a siege train and set off for Tyre, resuming the
strategy of capturing the cities of the coast. But Conrad had
stiffened the defences of Tyre considerably, and despite his well-
equipped and victorious army Saladin could not take the city.
Saladin brought with him Conrad's elderly father, William V of
Montferrat, who had been captured at Hattin, and offered his
release and great gifts if Conrad would surrender. The elderly
man, however, called upon his son to stand firm, whereupon
Conrad fired a crossbow at him. This may have been a bluff but it
worked and Saladin raised the siege, though his men seized
Beirut.[14] Saladin withdrew early in 1188 and then resumed his
attack on the coast in July. Tripoli, which had passed to Bohemond III of Antioch on the death of Raymond of Tripoli in late
1187, defied him successfully, in part because of the arrival of the
Sicilian fleet under the admiral Margaritus. Saladin then went
north into the principality of Antioch, capturing important places
like Laodicea and castles such as Saône and Bourzey. But he failed
to threaten Antioch itself, and his army was growing tired. In late
1188 Saladin concluded a truce with Bohemond III of Antioch.

By this time the storm that Saladin feared was already gathering
as Europe prepared for a crusade to regain what it had lost. In late
August 1187 Joscius, archbishop of Tyre, had been sent to tell

Europe of the disaster at Hattin and to ask for military assistance. The news had gone before him. When Pope Urban III (1185–7) was told of the disaster at Hattin on 20 October, he died of shock. His successor, Gregory VIII (October–December 1187) issued the papal bull *Audita tremendi*, calling for an immediate crusade. Clement III (1187–91) bent all his efforts to raising a new expedition to regain Jerusalem. On 27 March 1188 the Roman emperor Frederick Barbarossa (1152–89) took the cross, and in May 1189 set off down the Rhine from Regensburg at the head of an army, numbering perhaps 15,000 with 3,000 knights. What was most impressive about this army was its discipline. Frederick had been on the Second Crusade and witnessed the debacle of that expedition. He had learned his lesson well and refused to permit unarmed camp-followers or pilgrims in his host. He decreed that all should expect to be absent for two years and that even the poorest should provide for this by raising the substantial sum of 3 marks, and actually turned away men who did not meet this standard. He also prepared his route by establishing diplomatic relations with the states along the way. This was a well-equipped and tightly controlled army which inspired great fear in the Muslim world.

In January 1188, under the influence of the Church, the warring kings of England and France, Henry II (1152–89) and Philip Augustus (1179–1223), made peace and took the cross. They also agreed to the 'Saladin Tithe'. Essentially a form of income tax, it provided for every Christian to pay a tenth of his moveable wealth for the support of the Holy Land. But the war between England and France soon started up again. On 6 July 1189 Henry II died and was succeeded by his son Richard 'the Lionheart' (1189–99), who had to establish himself as king and come to terms with the

French. The two kings, deeply distrustful of one another, finally left Vézelay together on 4 July 1190—precisely three years after Hattin. Their armies formed the very heart of the Third Crusade.

Saladin was quite unable to take advantage of the long delay of the armies of the French and English kings because he had to guard against the arrival of Barbarossa who was marching through Anatolia. Moreover, now that he was no longer winning easy victories recruitment became more difficult. In the meantime a steady flow of reinforcement was arriving, notably a large force of Danish and Flemish ships. This made up for the loss of the Sicilians whose fleet withdrew as a result of the death of King William II (1166–89) without male heir and the ensuing succession crisis. Then a Pisan fleet arrived at Tyre on 6 April 1189. The newcomers were pleased to discover that Tyre was safe, but in time became irritated because nobody was offering to lead them against the enemy. In summer 1188 Saladin had freed King Guy. This was a skilful blow aimed at dividing his enemies. Most of the nobility of the old kingdom thought Guy had forfeited the crown and looked upon Conrad as their leader, pending the arrival of the western kings who would make a final settlement of the issue. Others, however, regarded Guy as a consecrated king, and amongst these was Bohemond III of Antioch to whom Raymond of Tripoli had bequeathed his great county. Guy was therefore able to find refuge in Tripoli, but he was locked out of Tyre which Conrad controlled. In late August Guy appeared before Tyre, appealed to the new forces encamped around the city, and suddenly marched south with them to besiege Acre. He arrived on 28 August, encamping about 1.5 kilometres away at Turon. Saladin immediately led his army towards the threatened city, but Guy's men in a well-entrenched camp could not be dislodged. Saladin was able to establish communications with his garrison in Acre and he started to use his fleet to supply the city. As Acre became the centre of the war, Conrad could hardly refuse to allow Tyre to be used as a base for the attack on Acre, so he and Guy patched up a peace. Guy was able to attract more troops arriving from the West to sustain the siege and bitter fighting raged around the city. Saladin was now paying for his failure to seize all the ports in 1187–8 and he had to guard against the imminent arrival of Frederick Barbarossa.

Saladin had pursued a policy of friendship with the Byzantines, who were in any case worried by the arrival of a German army, especially as Frederick was known to have been in contact with many of the rebellious peoples of the Balkans. However, despite Saladin's diplomatic approaches there is no real indication that Byzantium ever allied with him. The emperor Isaac Angelus obstructed Frederick as best he could, short of open war, but the sheer strength of the German force intimidated him. In March 1190 the Germans crossed the Bosphorus into Anatolia. At first the Germans expected the sultan of Iconium to give them free passage across his lands in Anatolia, but when this was refused they fought their way through, actually capturing the city of Iconium on 18 May. This was a remarkable demonstration of the fighting power of a well-disciplined western army. The Second Crusade had failed precisely because it lacked strong leadership and the coherence that came with it. It was with good reason that the Muslims trembled at the prospect of Barbarossa's arrival in Syria, but chance, always the arbiter of battle, intervened. On 10 June 1190 Barbarossa died in the Saleph River (modern Göksu, ancient Calycadnus). He may have drowned, or perhaps fallen in as a result of a heart attack. For the Muslims who were deeply worried by his approach this seemed like a divine delivery. In the words of Ibn al-Athir, one of Saladin's entourage, 'God saved us from this evil.'[15] The German army remained formidable, however, and command now devolved upon Barbarossa's son Frederick. But as they marched through friendly Armenian Cilicia to Antioch they were struck by a plague so that 'Disease and death fell upon them and they reached Antioch looking as though they had been exhumed from their graves'.[16]

As a result only a rump of Barbarossa's splendid army ever arrived in the Holy Land. The misfortune of the Germans was a great relief to Saladin because he had been forced to send troops into north Syria to contest their advance. He could now bring these back, and he launched attacks on King Guy's camp whenever the besiegers attacked Acre. As a result all such assaults failed, but the camp held out so that a stalemate resulted. The crusaders now awaited the arrival of the French and English kings while Saladin tried to rebuild his army to face their onslaught. One significant development was the death of Queen Sybil in the late autumn of 1190. Guy was king only by right of his wife, so his position was now precarious. Sybil's younger sister, Isabella, was now the heiress of the kingdom and Conrad of Montferrat persuaded the papal legate that her marriage to Humphrey of Toron was illicit and forced the hapless Humphrey to accept this. Conrad immediately married Isabella, making himself heir apparent.

The Muslims anticipated the arrival of Richard of England and Philip of France with some dread, and understood their threat:

This king of England was a mighty warrior of great courage and strong in purpose. He had much experience of fighting and was intrepid in battle, and yet he was in their eyes below the king of France in royal status, although being richer and more renowned for martial skill and courage.[17]

The tensions between these two leaders were immense. They had departed together from Vézelay in July 1190, only because neither trusted the other out of his sight. Their joint armies would have been an immense strain on the areas they crossed, so after agreeing to meet at Messina in Sicily Richard made for Marseilles, while Philip crossed the Alps to Genoa. By the time they got there William II of Sicily (1166–89) had died and a succession dispute had resulted in the weak rule of Tancred of Lecce. Richard and Philip were drawn into the conflict in the island, causing further delay to the crusade. Finally Philip gathered his men and they sailed quickly to Acre, arriving there on 20 April 1191.

By contrast, Richard's large fleet of 100 ships carrying about 8,000 troops was scattered by a storm. As a result of this, the ship bearing Richard's fiancée, Berengaria, found refuge off Limassol in Cyprus. The island was nominally part of the Byzantine empire, but its governor, Isaac Comnenus, had declared himself to be independent of distant Constantinople. He tried to seize Berengaria, presumably with the idea of holding her hostage. The lady refused to surrender herself and on 8 May Richard arrived with his fleet and army and was at first remarkably conciliatory. On 11 May a ship came from Acre carrying King Guy, his brother Geoffrey of Lusignan, and Bohemond III of Antioch. Richard was king of England, but he was also duke of Aquitaine, and in that capacity the Lusignans had been amongst his most important vassals. They seem to have persuaded Richard of the value of Cyprus to the Latin East, and reported that Isaac had been treating with Saladin. As a result Richard conquered the island. Isaac surrendered to Richard, and it is said that he begged not to be put in chains of iron. Richard agreed, and had him bound in chains of silver. Richard finally reached Acre on 11 June 1191. He and Philip embraced, but camped on opposite sides of the city. Relations between them were very strained, and when Philip mounted an attack on the city in late June Richard refused to let his men join in and the attempt failed. A little later Richard and his men tried to storm the city without French support, but got nowhere. However, the city walls were sadly battered and the garrison was near the end of its endurance.

After Hattin Saladin knew he had to seize the coastal cities, and he had bent considerable efforts to that end. But he had shrunk from the cost of assaulting the major centres of European power at Tripoli and Antioch and even Tyre. And he had failed to take decisive action when Guy besieged Acre. Now he could not defeat a formidable crusading army backed by a fleet. On 12 July 1191 the city surrendered. It was agreed that Saladin would release 1,500 crusader prisoners, return the 'True Cross' captured at Hattin, and pay 200,000 dinars in exchange for the lives and liberty of his Acre garrison. Hattin had seemed so decisive, but it was a victory in a battle, an episode which did not end the war. Saladin had failed to seize the coastal cities and now found himself on the defensive. The indecisiveness of Hattin doomed the Middle East to another century of warfare.

On 22 July King Philip announced his intention to return home. This was partly because he had been ill during the siege and partly because one of his great vassals, Count Philip of Flanders, had died at Acre and the fate of his huge fief was of deep concern to the French king. On 28 July the two kings announced a settlement of the kingship of Jerusalem. They agreed that Guy would remain as king of Jerusalem, but that on his death the succession would fall to Isabella, Conrad, and their heirs. Richard was now in undisputed command of the army. Richard was a highly sophisticated soldier, fully prepared to use diplomacy alongside armed might. Immediately after his arrival he had made contact with Saladin's brother, al-Adil who acted as a channel for diplomatic contact between the two sides. For his part, Saladin recognized that the military situation had turned against him, but he knew there was distrust in the crusader camp. The profits of the conquest of Acre were shared between the English and French kings, to the exclusion of the many others who had participated. Leopold of Austria, who led the rump of the German army, was infuriated when his standard was thrown from the ramparts and he was refused any share of the booty. Conrad of Montferrat had established his own contacts with Saladin while the French who had remained in Acre under the duke of Burgundy resented Richard.

Richard faced precisely the same military problem that had confronted Saladin before 1187. The Holy Land was anchored by cities now in Saladin's possession and he had a powerful field army to relieve any effort to besiege them. The Christians held only a tiny coastal enclave around Tyre and Acre, and Muslim possession of Sidon and Beirut meant they were cut off from contact by land with Tripoli and Antioch which were ruled by Bohemond III. Richard set out to seize the coastal cities, supported by a strong fleet. Saladin understood the situation and his first ploy was to procrastinate over the surrender terms agreed for Acre, thus delaying the Christian army. Richard recognized this gambit and on 20 August ordered the execution of all 2,600 of the Acre garrison in sight of the enemy army. At one stroke this served to avoid the problem of leaving fit prisoners behind and to vent the bloodlust of the army fanned by memories of Hattin and a long and bitter siege. Richard ruthlessly sacrificed these men to military expediency, but even Saladin's biographer recognized that this slaughter was partly the result of the sultan's deliberate prevarication:

> When the king of England saw that the Sultan hesitated to hand over money, the prisoners and the Cross, he dealt treacherously towards the Muslim prisoners....He had all the Frankish forces, horse and foot, march out at the time of the afternoon prayers on Tuesday 27 *rajab* [20 August]. They brought their tents forward as far as that and then moved on into the middle of the plain....The enemy then brought out the Muslim prisoners for whom God had decreed martyrdom, about 3000 bound in ropes. Then as one man they charged them with stabbings and blows with the sword they slew them in cold blood, while the Muslim advance guard watched.[18]

Richard was determined to seize Jaffa which would provide a base for a strike inland to Jerusalem. He had about 10,000 men at his disposal, but Saladin commanded roughly twice this number. On 25 August Richard assembled his army in much the same formation that Guy had adopted at Hattin. His cavalry were drawn up in three groups each of which was surrounded by infantry. Arrayed in these three boxes they began their march south. But unlike at Hattin Richard's fleet hovered offshore providing food and water. Moreover, although his infantry on the landward (left) side of the army were exposed to enemy assaults, Richard could rotate them to the shoreside, where they were virtually immune from attack, to give them rest. As at Hattin on 3 July, Saladin savagely harassed his enemy and both sides suffered heavy casualties. Saladin's biographer described with admirable clarity the military situation as Richard moved south:

> The Muslims were shooting arrows on their flanks, trying to incite them to break ranks, while they controlled themselves severely and covered the route in this way, travelling very steadily as their ships moved along at sea opposite them, until they completed each stage and camped.[19]

As at Hattin, Saladin was trying to erode the crusader army to the point where he could destroy it in pitched battle. The fighting was savage, partly because in retaliation for the massacre of the Acre garrison, Saladin had ordered that no prisoners be taken. Baha al-Din remarked on one captive who had a 'perfect frame with such elegance of body and refinement of manners', but he was decapitated. Several others suffered the same fate, notably a group of fourteen including a woman.[20] But the outstanding factor was the discipline of the crusader army under a leader whom they trusted. Most of Richard's own troops, who formed the core of his force, consisted of mercenaries, both horse and foot; well equipped and steady, they set an example to the rest of the army as even their enemies noted with admiration:

> The enemy army was already in formation with the infantry surrounding it like a wall, wearing solid iron corselets and full-length well-made chain-mail, so that arrows were falling on them with no effect...I saw various individuals amongst the Franks with ten arrows fixed in their backs, pressing on in this fashion quite unconcerned.[21]

Richard's objective, the port of Jaffa, was some 128 kilometres from Acre. From there an attack on Jerusalem could be supplied by sea. But his army was making slow progress in the scorching weather and the heat of Muslim attack. Saladin, however, had his own problems. His army was suffering heavy casualties and, all too obviously, was not preventing the enemy advance. Muslim armies were good at harassment, but Saladin knew that if Richard's knightly cavalry struck the mass of his army he would be defeated, and south of Arsuf the coastal plain narrowed, making his tactics of manoeuvre and harassment more difficult. On 5 September negotiations between Saladin and Richard were resumed, but the English king demanded, as he always had, the full restoration of the kingdom of Jerusalem. On 7 September Saladin deployed his army for battle in the plain near Arsuf. Richard adjusted the pattern of his troops, dividing his cavalry into five units, presumably for flexibility, but he continued his march, drawing Saladin's army into the narrower areas to the south where they would be vulnerable to a counter-charge. Richard undoubtedly hoped to keep his cavalry in hand until the opportunity arose for a decisive assault which would destroy his enemy. In the event his rearguard, manned by the orders, was so mauled that they attacked on their own and he was forced to release the rest of his force lest they be destroyed. The impact of these attacks upon the Muslim army was immense:

The enemy's situation worsened still more and the Muslims thought they had them in their power. Eventually the first detachments of their infantry reached the plantations of Arsuf. Then their cavalry massed together and agreed on a charge, as they feared for their people and thought that only a charge would save them. I saw them grouped together in the middle of the foot-soldiers. They took their lances and gave a shout as one man. The infantry opened gaps for them and they charged in unison. One group charged our right wing, another our left, and the third our centre. It happened that I was in the centre which took to wholesale flight. My intention was to join the left wing, since it was nearer to me. I reached it after it had been broken utterly, so I thought to join the right wing, but then I saw that it had fled more calamitously than all the rest.[22]

Saladin's army was not totally destroyed, but its morale was badly shaken and from this time on he hesitated to face Richard in the open field. Moreover, the tough soldiers who served him had come for booty: failure could make future recruitment very difficult. Richard was a stranger to the East, yet he had skilfully adopted an alien formation, the fighting march, and made it work. The contrast with Hattin was remarkable. There Guy's army had begun to fall apart in a mere 4 kilometres of march after Turan, but Richard's men endured fourteen days of attacks over 100 kilometres. Richard had carefully taken into account problems of supply, which Guy had not. The contrast in outcomes points to the difference between the commanders and the respect in which they were held.

On 10 September Richard reached Jaffa. The cement which held his army together was Jerusalem, but Richard as a military man had doubts about attacking the city. He and the senior barons of Jerusalem and the orders knew that even if the city could be captured, holding it posed insuperable difficulties once the bulk of the crusaders had gone home. He first proposed that the army go on to seize Ascalon: this would give total command of the coast and interrupt Saladin's communications with Egypt. Saladin, hearing of this, immediately ordered that the city be abandoned and its fortifications destroyed. Even more ambitiously, Richard discussed the possibility of using the fleet for a direct attack upon Egypt. Diplomatic negotiations with Saladin's brother, al-Adil, continued, and the idea was floated that the

Christians should hold the coast and enjoy access to Jerusalem under the sovereignty of al-Adil. There is even a story that, as part of the agreement, al-Adil would marry Richard's sister Joanna, who is said to have been enraged by the idea of being married off to an infidel!

At the same time Saladin was negotiating with Conrad who was hoping to establish a state of his own, probably in what is now Lebanon. In the end, interesting as the various possibilities were, Richard had no choice but to attack Jerusalem if he were to hold his army together because most of the crusaders had come to liberate the Holy City and wanted nothing to do with other objectives. On 31 October the whole crusading army set out towards Jerusalem, but the advance was very slow because Richard insisted on taking various strongholds to guard his communications. By Christmas the crusaders had reached Latrun in the Judaean foothills. The winter was harsh, and although by early January 1192 they were only 19 kilometres from Jerusalem at Bayt Nuba, the decision in the end was taken to retreat, with a resultant slump in morale: 'then was the army which had been so eager in its advance, so discouraged, that not since God created time was there ever seen an army so dejected and so depressed, so disturbed and so astounded, nor so overcome with great sadness'.[23]

Richard then turned to seize and refortify Ascalon which is what he had wanted in the first place, but essentially a stalemate persisted. Much of the army was restive, and in Acre the factions of Guy and Conrad were coming to blows. With problems multiplying in England, Richard started to think about a settlement. In April he agreed that Conrad should be recognized as king of Jerusalem. Guy was compensated by being made ruler of Cyprus which his descendants would rule until 1474. Richard had already sold the island to the Templars for 100,000 *besants*, but their administration of the island was incompetent. When they returned it to him, he refused to surrender the 40,000 deposit which they had given him. He now sold the island again to King Guy who paid him 60,000 'up front' and promised a further 40,000 which he never paid. On 28 April 1192 Conrad was murdered by the Assassins. Some said this was at the behest of Richard, but Conrad had many enemies, and ultimately this paved the way for a settlement. All parties agreed to the marriage of an important crusader leader, Henry, count of Champagne, to Queen Isabella. On 22 May Richard seized Darum to the south of Ascalon, completing control of the Palestinian littoral, but despite his reservations, the leaders of his army resolved on another attempt on Jerusalem. This time they reached Bayt Nuba in five days, but the attack stalled as the leaders debated the next step. In the event a committee appointed by Richard resolved not to press on to Jerusalem, and the army retreated; in the process the French, who had always wanted to go on to Jerusalem, broke away.

Despite intensive negotiations, the stalemate continued until July 1192 by which time Saladin had built up his army once more. Although Saladin was somewhat reluctant, the leaders of his army decided to profit from Richard's absence at Acre by making a surprise attack on Jaffa on 28 July. The city fell quickly and the Turks even got a foothold in the citadel when on 1 August Richard returned by sea. He ordered his ships to beach and leaped off, sword in hand to lead a charge which broke into the city and joined up with the garrison of the citadel. The Muslims were put to flight, but even when he was joined by Henry of Champagne Richard's force was heavily outnumbered, for he had only 55 knights and 2,000 foot. Saladin returned to the attack on 4 August and surprised Richard, once more breaking into the town whose fortifications were by now badly weakened. But Richard rallied his forces, forming a hedgehog with his spearmen:

> they placed their right knee on the ground and fixed the toes of their right foot in the soil and held the left foot forward with the left knee bent. They held a buckler in front of them in their left hand, or a targe or some other type of shield. In their right hand they held a lance, with the blunt end fixed into the ground and the sharp end with its iron head pointing forward threateningly towards the attacking enemy. The king, who was very skilled in warfare, placed a crossbow-man between each two who were protecting themselves with their shields like this, and another person next to him who could keep pulling back the crossbow quickly. So one person had the job of loading crossbows while other kept firing bolts.[24]

This formation held off the Muslims and when they were weakened by their losses, Richard led his tiny force of knights in a great charge which routed the enemy. This was a personal triumph for Richard whose bravery set an astonishing example to all, so that at the end, 'The king's body was completely covered with darts, which stuck out like the spines of a hedgehog. His horse was also bristling with the countless arrows which were stuck in its trappings. Thus this extraordinary knight returned from the contest.'[25]

The battle raised crusader morale and was a bitter failure for Saladin, but its result did not alter the strategic situation and essentially confirmed the stalemate which had existed for some time. Fresh negotiations were now opened and on 2 September culminated in the Treaty of Jaffa between Saladin and Richard. A three-year truce was concluded which was to cover Antioch and Tripoli as well as Jerusalem. The kingdom was to hold Acre and a shallow coastal strip down to Jaffa, but the fortifications of Ascalon were to be destroyed. The inland area around Ramla was to be jointly ruled and Christians were guaranteed free access to Jerusalem. Richard left Acre on 9 October 1192, never to return: the Third Crusade was over and there was no lack of critics for its failure to capture Jerusalem. But it was also a setback for Saladin, and one that has, as we shall see, profoundly affected his reputation in the Islamic world.

Western people were disappointed by the outcome of the Third Crusade even though it had re-established Christian rule in the Holy Land. This was only a small coastal enclave and the enormous effort of the crusade had failed to liberate Jerusalem. This new kingdom of Jerusalem, despite many problems, proved remarkably resilient and lasted until 1291. At the same time Muslims were disappointed at the ultimate outcome of Hattin. Far from ending the western incursion into the Middle East it triggered a crescendo of crusades determined to reconquer Jerusalem: the Third (1187–92), as we have seen, created a new and smaller Latin kingdom of Jerusalem.

Moreover, the failure of the Third Crusade left Europeans to reflect on strategy. The First Crusade had gone pell-mell for Jerusalem, and circumstances at that time had favoured such temerity. On the Third Crusade many had still believed that this was the right thing to do. However, the outcome of the crusade showed that things had changed. Richard the Lionheart had wanted to attack Egypt because it was the centre of Saladin's power, and the strength of western naval power meant that it was very vulnerable. New political circumstances made this a very attractive possibility in the thirteenth century. The death of Saladin in 1193 led to quarrelling amongst the Ayyubid family for control of his empire. Most commonly his lands were divided between Syria and Egypt whose rulers then fought one another for control of the whole. These divisions clearly made Richard's strategy appealing and offered hope to westerners eager to reconquer Jerusalem. The Fourth Crusade (1202–4) intended to attack Egypt but was diverted by a series of chance events to Constantinople. However the Fifth Crusade (1217–21) attacked and seized the important Egyptian port of Damietta, prompting the sultan to offer return of the city of Jerusalem in exchange for an evacuation of the city. This was refused and the crusading army was ultimately defeated, though only with difficulty. On the Sixth Crusade (1228–9) the emperor Frederick II of Hohenstaufen (1214–50) exploited the conflict between Syria and Egypt to achieve a truce by which the sultan of Egypt surrendered Jerusalem and much of the old kingdom to the Christians. The Crusade of the Barons (1239–41) played off Syria and Egypt and managed to extend Christian control of the Holy City until 1244 when the Egyptian sultan enlisted the aid of the Khwarezmians, a rootless Turkish horde from the southern steppe, who besieged and sacked Jerusalem inflicting terrible damage on the holy city. This provoked the Crusade of St Louis, king of France (1248–54) which repeated the strategy of the Fifth Crusade and seized Damietta. However, Louis's attempt to capture Cairo was crushed in the tangle of waterways which formed the Nile Delta.

This crescendo of crusading, which was the consequence of Hattin, had lasting effects in the Middle East. In 1250, exasperated by the divisions of the Ayyubids, their slave-soldiers, the Mamluks, overthrew their masters and set up their own Mamluk kingdom which was devoted to *jihad* against all unbelievers and which would last until the sixteenth century. The Mamluks were Turks and related people, and they recruited their army from amongst the young warriors of the steppe lands from which they orginated. The Mamluk leaders equipped and disciplined them to create a formidable standing army which was sustained by savage exploitation of the Egyptian people. The leading warlords amongst the Mamluks formed a kind of military republic and they elected (and deposed) one of their own as sultan. These highly disciplined soldiers of God destroyed the last strongholds of Latin rule in Palestine, until in 1291 they seized and destroyed Acre and ended two centuries of crusader incursions. A century of bitter warfare after Hattin shattered the Holy Land and left its cities in ruins. The decision of the Mamluks to destroy all the cities of the Palestinian coast in order to deny their use to any future crusade, condemned the hinterland to being a backwater for centuries. But what is insufficiently appreciated is how far Hattin helped to usher in a new world in the Mediterranean.

The Latin kingdom offered a base for the new crusades which were increasingly better organized and financed, because Pope Innocent III (1198–1216), spurred on by the desire to regain Jerusalem, reformed crusading. He allowed men and women who could not travel personally to pay and thereby gain a spiritual reward which was now defined much more closely than ever before. He instituted systematic mass preaching, and fostered ceremonies which kept the memory of Jerusalem alive. He began regular taxation of the clergy to raise funds for the expeditions to the East. Under Innocent it became clear that crusading was a papal institution controlled and directed by the pope. Even though the expeditions of the thirteenth century increasingly attacked Egypt, they were accompanied by fighting in the Holy

Land. In Italy Richard's excursion into Sicily weakened the regime of King Tancred whose dynasty did not outlast his death in 1193. Richard's long absence in the Holy Land enabled his enemy, Philip Augustus of France, to undermine and weaken his dominions in Normandy, the Loire, Brittany, and southern France. Despite his military genius Richard was never able to restore his power fully, and after his death King John (1199–1216) inherited a weakened state and ultimately lost much of it to Philip Augustus.

Hattin had enormous repercussions for Byzantium. After the death of the emperor Manuel in 1180 Byzantium underwent a series of political coups, most notably in 1185 when Isaac Angelus (1185–1204) mounted the throne. The conflicts at Constantinople triggered rebellions in the Balkans and Bulgaria and when Frederick Barbarossa, on the Third Crusade, forced his way through the empire against the wishes of Isaac, its weaknesses became very apparent. In 1195 Isaac was deposed, blinded, and imprisoned by his brother, Alexius III Angelus (reigned 1195–1203). In 1202 another crusade was launched to recover Jerusalem, but its leaders, lured by the riches and weakness of Byzantium, captured Constantinople and established a new Latin empire, supported by the Venetians. However, Latin rule was deeply resented by the Greek population, and as a result this new Latin empire lacked strength. Eventually the remaining fragments of the Byzantine lands unified and recaptured Constantinople in 1261, though this restored empire was a mere shadow of its former self.

Hattin, therefore, was an immensely important battle with repercussions across the whole Mediterranean and beyond. The battle itself was an important episode, a great victory, in the wars of the crusades. But it was not decisive. Saladin could not strike at the bases of crusading in Europe, and he failed even to seize the cities of the Palestinian coast. To later generations of Muslims Hattin seemed like a victory wasted, with consequent effects upon Saladin's reputation in the Islamic world. It was also a victory soon forgotten, though for very different reasons, in East and West.

# 5

# Hattin Today

## A Poisoned Heritage

For Europeans the memory of Hattin as a battle has been almost entirely eclipsed by the myth of Saladin transformed truly into a 'veray parfit gentil knight'.[1] It is remarkable that nearly 800 years after his death Saladin is remembered to a remarkable extent amongst the very peoples whose Christian aspirations he had so effectively tried to destroy. Type in 'Saladin' on the Internet and innumerable entries appear. Refine that to consider books and there is truly a plethora. A few are academic studies, but most are popular works and novels. There is even a *Saladin Trilogy* by the author Jack Hight. In French the first few chapters of David Camus's novel *Les Chevaliers du royaume* (*Knights of the Kingdom*) depict the aftermath of the battle, through the eyes of a captured Hospitaller knight. A Swedish trilogy by Jan Guillou depicts the fictitious Arn Magnusson who was forced to become a Templar knight. In the final volume, *The Kingdom at Road's End* Arn is wounded and captured at Hattin, but saved by the intercession of Saladin.

And for the most part these entries and works are of western origin and are admiring rather than condemnatory. Their sheer scale shows that knowledge of Saladin and admiration for him reaches far beyond any literary elite. Saladin has appeared in many western films, generally portrayed in a sympathetic light. This was certainly true of Cecil B. DeMille's 1935 epic *The Crusades*, and the 1954 *King Richard and the Crusaders*. In *Kingdom of Heaven* (2005) Jerusalem is presented as an island of tolerance ruined by a few fanatics like King Guy and Reynald of Châtillon, and Saladin appears as a personification of modeation, albeit one on the opposite side. In a rather different vein, in 1947 Alvis began to design a new armoured car for the British army—a formidable six-wheeler with a 76-mm gun which entered service in 1958— and they called it the Saladin. In the 1980s 'Saladin Security' worked with the extreme right-wing 'Contras' in Nicaragua and still operates as 'International Security and Risk Management Solutions' in London. These uses reflect the resonances of his name, and its association with victory and military prestige. How has this come about, and why has the memory of Hattin, Saladin's greatest victory, been largely forgotten?

Before 1187 Saladin was deeply hated as a threat to the Latin kingdom. William of Tyre, the great chronicler of the Latin East who died in 1184, regarded him as a dire menace to the settler states, and portrayed him as a usurper who had displaced and perhaps murdered Nur ad-Din's sons. Many of those who fought against him, like the anonymous writer of the *De Expugnatione Terrae Sanctae Libellus* who had helped to defend Jerusalem in 1187, regarded the outcome of the battle as deeply shaming:

> What can I say? It would be more fitting to weep and wail than to say anything. Alas! Should I describe with impure lips how the precious wood of the Lord, our redeemer, was seized by the damnable hands

of the damned? Woe to me that in the days of my miserable life
I should be forced to see such things.[2]

Very shortly after the fall of Jerusalem Saladin was demonized in
an Old French poem which portrayed him as a bastard of Nur ad-
Din who may have been the lover of his father's wife, and related
a story that he killed a caliph who opposed him with a blow of a
hammer. One of the pieces in the famous collection of satirical
and bawdy student songs, the *Carmina Burana*, compiled by 1230
but incorporating much earlier material, attacks Saladin as a thief
and destroyer of the land. Church writers of the thirteenth and
fourteenth centuries, inspired by theological hatred, usually continued this demonization of the victor of Hattin. But a very
different and much more influential memorialization of Saladin
emerged, almost entirely in Old French, the vernacular language
of the ruling classes of western Europe.

These people, the aristocracy and knights of the West, were
developing a taste for romances, stories in which the classic
canons of fiction, characterization, and narrative tension, were
evident. Such tales were all the better for an exotic setting, and yet
they had to embody the military values of the code of chivalry
which was so important to their audience. These were the very
people who supported the crusade and who made pilgrimages to
the Latin kingdom of Jerusalem, and its only great city, Acre.
There they came into contact with a view of the recent past which
presented Saladin in a sympathetic light, and softened the harsh-
ness of the memory of Hattin. Pilgrimage was in many ways a
form of medieval tourism, and Acre did a good business in
souvenirs. At the lowest level humble men and women bought
simple lead badges, but for the rich and powerful there were

rather more sophisticated offerings. In the early decades of the thirteenth century, as the kingdom recovered from Hattin, the great history of William of Tyre, which was ended by its author's death in 1184, was translated into Old French. By about 1230 the story was brought up to date from 1184 by the *Continuations*, which were themselves subsequently updated in various versions as time went on. We do not know who produced the original translations or who wrote the *Continuations*, but they seem to have originated in commercial circles. Writing offices at Acre produced manuscripts which rich pilgrims could buy and take back to the West. The unknown writers, therefore, had to cater for the tastes of their clientele, and at the same time bear in mind the political environment in which they lived and worked.

By the time such works were composed, politics in the Latin kingdom had, to use a modern phrase, 'moved on'. The bitterness of defeat at Hattin was a thing of the past. Moreover, nobody had much interest in pursuing a blame game for such a distant event. In 1187 the Ibelins and Guy of Lusignan had been enemies, but by the 1230s Guy's descendants (the Lusignans) were kings of Cyprus and the Ibelins were great barons in both Cyprus and the Holy Land. When the Hohenstaufen emperor Frederick II (1212–50) became king of Jerusalem in the 1220s and tried to enforce his power over Cyprus and the kingdom, he united these former enemies against him in a long civil war in the 1230s and 1240s. At that time, when the *Continuations* were being produced, it was, therefore, better by far to agree that the loss of the kingdom was God's punishment for the sins of the settlers, so that in placing blame on everbody nobody stood out at fault. In fact the *Continuations* offer a kind of supernatural excuse for the defeat of Hattin and the victory of Saladin. Before the battle they recount that some sergeants who served in Balian of Ibelin's rearguard discovered an old Saracen woman who confessed to casting a spell on the army of Jerusalem, such that even if they had stayed at Saffuriyah they would have been defeated. This story is then verified by reference to the biblical tale of Balaam's ass. This story takes up more space than any of the accounts of the Battle of Hattin itself. This elaboration of the incident points to its importance in the minds of those who composed it, for the clear implication of this was that defeat was inevitable, rather than a mistake in judgement in particular circumstances for which any particular person could be held responsible. It is notable also that one important version of the *Continuations* mentions neither the killing of the members of the orders who had been captured at Hattin, nor Saladin's refusal to take prisoners during Richard's march down to Arsuf.

In addition these Old French texts cast a very favourable light on certain generous acts of Saladin, notably to the Ibelins. As we have seen, Saladin had very strong political reasons for treating the surviving leaders of the Jerusalemite aristocracy well. Saladin agreed to free the Ibelin children at the start of the siege of Jerusalem, and in the *Continuations* this is introduced in a very striking way: 'I must not omit to tell you about an act of courtesy of Saladin's during the siege of Jerusalem.'[3] To attribute this to courtesy, rather than the political desire of Saladin to draw the nobility into a web of defeatism, deflected attention from Balian of Ibelin's narrow pursuit of his family's concerns. The same language is used about Saladin's decision, at the request of their wives, to free some of the knights captured at Hattin. And the language is very important. The Old French *courtoisie* is not quite what is implied by the modern English word 'courtesy', for the word essentially means related to the court, that is to high status and the idealized behaviour associated with it. In the Jerusalem of the 1230s when the *Continuations* were written the question of the Ibelin relationship with Saladin needed to be handled carefully. And these writers generally present Saladin as behaving very well towards the people of Jerusalem after the surrender of the city. More particularly they underline the contrast between the Christian lord of Nephim, who robbed the refugees from the city, and Saladin, who had those sent to Alexandria treated with great kindness. All this served to justify not just Balian of Ibelin's relations with Saladin, but also the whole habit of negotiating with Saladin's descendants, the Ayyubids, which was so common by the time the *Continuations* were written.

What we see, therefore, in these histories, which were immensely popular in the West, is an evolving and distinctly softening view of Saladin, quite at odds with the spirit of crusade. This certainly suited the political conditions of the kingdom in the thirteenth century. But the transformation of Saladin and the memory of Hattin also catered for the tastes of the writers' market, the European aristocrats and knights. The European upper class was becoming more sophisticated and more educated, and this literature took up a very common theme—those who waged war liked to feel that they had a worthy opponent and this sometimes transcended religion. Even at the time of the First Crusade in 1097, on the occasion of the first battle between the Turks and a western army, one of the knights who took part commented:

> What man, however experienced and learned, would dare to write of the skill and prowess and courage of the Turks...They have a saying

that they are of common stock with the Franks, and that no man, except the Franks and themselves, are naturally born to be knights.[4]

In Saladin western writers of courtly literature discerned an individual with all the qualities of a great opponent, at a time when the output of vernacular literature was increasing enormously. Moreover, any recitation of the facts of his life revealed traits of behaviour which could easily be idealized. Most particularly there was his kindness to Eschiva of Tiberias after Hattin, to Balian of Ibelin at the siege of Jerusalem, and his concern to find husbands for the bereaved ladies of Jerusalem. Taken out of their particular context, these acts formed the raw material for the portrait of a really heroic and courteous enemy. We can see this mythologization of Saladin in a very complete form in an Old French poem of about 1250–60, the anonymous *Ordene de chevalerie*. In this poem a knight, Hugh of Tiberias, is captured in battle by Saladin who treats him very well, but demands to be told all the secrets of knighthood. Hugh protests at first that this is impossible because Saladin is not a Christian, but under pressure agrees and explains all to Saladin. As a necessary part of this, Saladin is portrayed in a highly favourable light, for at the end of his course of instruction he remits Hugh's ransom and permits him to go free, so that although at the start of the poem we are presented with an enemy of Christendom:

> A great lord of days gone by;
> He was full loyal Saracen
> And his name hight Saladin.
> Cruel he was, and did great scathe
> Full many times unto our faith, And to our folk did mickle ill
> Through pride of heart and evil will.

by the end we are told that:

> Of Saladin great praise had he
> Whereas he found his valiancy:
> Also he made him honoured fair
> Whereas he wrought with pain and care
> After his might good works to win.[5]

This mythologization of Saladin was given a special impulse by the circumstances of the Third Crusade. In retrospect this appeared as a duel between the towering personalities of Richard of England and Saladin and indeed the story of Richard and Saladin actually jousting became very popular in the thirteenth century and is pictured on the famous Chertsey Abbey tile. Soon after his death in 1199 Richard became a figure of myth and poetry, hence he figures in the Robin Hood legends. His glowing image necessarily illuminated that of Saladin. This highly personalized vision of the Third Crusade was spiced with much human and even erotic appeal. For, as we have noted, Richard had pursued his end of the liberation of the Holy Land by diplomacy as well as by war. Out of this arose the delightful picture of the two champions face to face, although actually they conducted their discussions through intermediaries and never met. But the whole story of the secret negotiations was given piquancy by the supposed involvement of Richard's sister, Joanna, who may at one time have been offered in marriage to Saladin's brother. These are the themes which dominate the literary picture of Saladin which became so elaborate in Europe.

In *Le Pas Saladin*, which appears to date from the thirteenth century, Saladin is portrayed as a chivalrous and noble leader who confronts the French army in a narrow pass. The story seems to have been very popular because Henry III ordered a painting of it in 1251 for Clarendon Palace. A number of pictures drawn from the story are known, and in his will of 1376 the Black Prince bequeathed a tapestry version. In the recital of the Minstrel of Rheims, dating from about 1260, Saladin is portrayed as having been a baptized Christian, though he hid this carefully. Some late medieval satires against clerical corruption show him being put off conversion by the wickedness of the clergy. Romances sometimes narrated fanciful tales of Saladin travelling to Europe and even having affairs with various notable ladies. He is mentioned kindly in Dante's *Inferno* (*c.*1314), by Juan Manuel in *El Conde Lucanor* (1335), and Boccaccio in his *Decameron* (1348–53). Lope de Vega gave a highly sympathetic portrayal in his play *Jerusalén Conquitada* (1604).

It has to be stressed that until the eighteenth century the crusade was a living concern for Europeans. From the fourteenth century the Ottoman Turks were seeking to conquer eastern and central Europe. In the sixteenth century their fleet tried to dominate the western basin of the Mediterranean. The threat of an Ottoman conquest of central Europe only really receded after their army failed to capture Vienna in 1683. Crusades in the defence of Europe continued, therefore, well beyond the Middle Ages, so that 1714 can be said to mark their end. All this gave Saladin a contemporary relevance which kept his memory, in its mythologized form, alive. In the eighteenth century the thinkers of the Age of the Enlightenment regarded crusading as a thing of the past, a deplorable aspect of obscurantist religion, which was widely condemned. But their condemnations ensured that crusading was not forgotten, and in the person of the mythologized

Saladin Enlightenment writers saw an opponent of crusading, a perfect representative of their modern attitudes. Voltaire in his *Essai sur les mœurs* portrayed Saladin as a model of eighteenth-century tolerance, a devout Muslim respectful of Christian belief, who triumphed over the ignorant and fanatical crusaders, and this vision of him was dramatized by Lessing in his play *Nathan the Wise*.

The Romantics did nothing to change this view of Saladin. Sir Walter Scott in *The Talisman* of 1825 was deeply laudatory. In his introduction Scott remarked:

> The period relating more immediately to the crusades, which I at last fixed upon, was that at which the warlike character of Richard I, wild and generous, a pattern of chivalry, with all its extravagant virtues, and its no less absurd error, was opposed to that of Saladin, in which the Christian and English monarch showed all the cruelty and violence of an Eastern Sultan, and Saladin on the other hand, displayed the deep policy and prudence of a European sovereign, whilst each contended which should excel the other in the knightly qualities of bravery and generosity.

This view of Saladin was certainly not confined to English-language countries, for when Kaiser Wilhelm II of Germany (1888–1918) visited Damascus in 1898 he was horrified to discover the poor state of the great hero's tomb which he restored at his own expense. It had its effect even on serious academic writing, for its influence is very evident in S. Lane-Poole's *Saladin and the Fall of the Kingdom of Jerusalem* of 1898 which was, until quite recently, the standard English-language biography of Saladin. In 1968 the distinguished Arabic historian P. K. Hitti, repeated the romantic picture in his *Makers of Arab History* when he described Saladin: 'His manners were those of a gentleman, considerate, unostentatious, and abstemious ... Power and gentleness, author-ity and magnanimity seem to have found in him a happy and rare combination.'[6]

Such reverential treatment has been superseded by recent aca-demic studies which have been more balanced. Overall there can be no doubt that Saladin was a man who had, by the standards of the day, strong humanitarian instincts. However, he was the prisoner of a complex political situation which on many occa-sions overrode his personal preferences. In popular literature, however, and above all in novels and plays the rosy vision of the great and generous Islamic leader has persisted.[7]

Although the Saladin myth has drowned out the memory of Hattin, the battle is the very foundation of Saladin's fame, for without it he would be largely unknown. The European myth of Saladin arose from the desire amongst the military aristocracy to show the victor as a worthy, indeed praiseworthy, opponent who, underneath it all, is 'one of us' in some sense. It is a kind of compensatory myth and one with remarkable persistence. But the power of the Saladin myth has recently stimulated popular explor-ation of his life. Hattin is such a dramatic event that it provides an important episode in the numerous modern novels covering the period, although it has never been important in western films. In the most recent, *Kingdom of Heaven*, it received only a distant long-shot. In a wider perspective, because Hattin is one of the supposed sites of the Sermon on the Mount, there is nothing odd in its featuring on the well-publicized 'Jesus Trail' across Galilee, or the naming of a Mount Hattin church in Baltimore. Nor, given the need to exploit the tourist trade, is it odd that there is an annual re-enactment of the battle in Israel. Other manifestations of its imprint on western culture are perhaps more surprising.

There are numerous postings on YouTube and elsewhere on the Internet in which private individuals, using a wide variety of European languages, feel the need to tell the story of the battle. One website, for example, features a lively debate on whether the Christian defeat at Hattin was inevitable.[8] Sometimes Hattin is retold through the medium of film, though in general these are no more than a series of stills strung together by a voice-over commentary. For the most part these retellings of the battle have no obvious propaganda purpose; the story is simply told from a standard western viewpoint, though the History of Palestine website has a version which provides a distinctively Muslim stance. It is perhaps less surprising that a substantial number of computer games are built around the battle, notably by Heaven-Games, Total War, and Warcraft, for after all there are only so many medieval battles which can provide good stories. However, it is strange to discover that there is an Austrian pop group, 'an extreme epic metal band', with the name 'Horns of Hattin'. Then there are the 'Templars' who have issued an album called the *Horns of Hattin*, and the 'Crusader Kings' whose release is entitled *Horns of Hattin and Aftermath*. Another group, the Weedybeats, produced an orchestral piece simply called *Hattin*. Perhaps the most ambitious ensemble is Crystallion whose *Hattin Album* is a kind of oratorio of the battle, with songs put into the mouths of King Guy and Reynald of Châtillon.

Hattin has left an imprint on western culture but it is even deeper amongst the peoples of the Middle East. Kurdish attitudes towards Saladin are, to say the least, ambivalent. On the one hand he is the most famous of all Kurds, and his golden eagle is the symbol of the Kurdish Regional Government in Turkey. On the other, Kurds have no nation of their own and resent the

Arabization of their hero. So there is pride as illustrated by one YouTube posting of September 2012—'The Turks are jealous because he was a Kurd'—but another praises him as a noble leader 'except for choosing Islam over Kurdishness.'

For Jews, particularly Israelis, the memory of the crusades poses painful dilemmas. Their general alignment is western, and the parallels between Israel and the Latin kingdom are very obvious. But for them there can be no simple identification with the usual western accounts, because Jews were so often victims of departing crusaders determined to wipe out the 'enemy within' before departing for the Holy Land. The novelist Amos Oz bases his 1971 *Unto Death* around the crusades and uses their fanaticism to show how Jews need to cling to rationalism as providing their best path to the future. In a not dissimilar vein there is a touching poem by Dahlia Ravikovitch, 'The Horns of Hittin', which suggests a plague on both your houses:

> A curving scimitar burst from the East
> like a Jester's staff.
> Saladin advanced from the East in gaudy colours.
> With the horns of a wild beast
> he gored them hip and thigh, that infidel dog:
> Saladin
> did them in
> at the Horns of Hittin.
>
> No kingdom remained to them,
> no life eternal,
> no Jerusalem.
> How cruel and naive the crusaders were.
> They plundered everything.[9]

But it is for the Arabs that Hattin has its most vigorous afterlife and the greatest impact upon modern politics. At the same time its memory is deeply divisive. Saladin's life and deeds were celebrated by his biographers, Qadi al-Fadil from Ascalon, Imad al-Din of Isfahan, and Baha al-Din from Mosul. The historian Ibn al-Athir (1160–1233), although a Kurd who worked in Saladin's army, was more sceptical because he had a special devotion to the Zengid clan, but even he spoke of Saladin's glorious deeds. Ibn Abi Tay (1160–1234), was a Shi'ite, yet just as admiring of Saladin as most of his Sunni contemporaries. But the mainstream of Shi'ite opinion reflects the views of the Shi'ite jurist Abu Turab (1132–1217), who remembered that in 1171 Saladin had extinguished the Shi'ite Fatimid caliphate of Cairo: 'may God not be pleased with Salah al-Din. He is *fasad al-din* (destruction of the faith), he expelled the [Fatimid] Caliphs from Egypt'.[10] Abi Tay never blamed Saladin for this act. However, it should be remembered that during the twelfth century the Fatimids lost both prestige and followers even amongst their own Ismaili tradition, and Abi Tay belonged to the Twelvers, a rival faction of the Shia, who viewed the Fatimids with hostility as pretenders. The Sunni–Shi'ite division of Islam is the basic cleavage in the remembrance of Saladin and Hattin. The great Muslim historian Abu Shamah (1203–68) wrote a history of Nur al-Din and Saladin which portrays them as a succession of true Sunni leaders, champions of orthodoxy and scourges of the Shi'ites as well as victors over the crusaders. This explicitly Sunni and anti-Shi'ite interpretation of Saladin was enormously amplified in the fourteenth century by writers such as Ibn Taymiyah (1263–1328) and through them Sunni triumphalism passed into modern writings.

In fact Saladin and Hattin seem largely to have dropped out of Muslim consciousness after the thirteenth century. In the fourteenth century they were remembered in a few accounts, but Ibn

Khaldun, one of the greatest of Arab historians, referred to Saladin only in passing in his magnificent history, the *Muqaddimah*. Perhaps Saladin's reputation suffered somewhat because the result of Hattin seemed so meagre. Moreover, his memory may have been harmed because of the behaviour of his descendants, the Ayyubids. They partitioned his empire between Egypt and Syria, and quarrelled amongst themselves, enabling the tiny kingdom of Jerusalem to enjoy a fairly comfortable existence. Even worse, in 1229 the German emperor Frederick II (1214–50) adroitly exploited the disputes between Egypt and Syria to take Jerusalem back again for the crusader kingdom by dint of diplomacy. The bickering of the Ayyubids meant that they could never really generate the spirit of *jihad* to clothe the dynasty in glory. All this was ultimately a result of the limitations of Saladin's achievement, the limitations in fact of Hattin, because Saladin failed to expel the westerners from the Middle East. It is significant that the ruthless and triumphant Egyptian Mamluk sultan Baybars (1260–77) was commemorated in a popular Egyptian folklore poem, *Sirat al-Zahir Baibars*. The Mamluk sultans, backed by their remarkable army, went on to proclaim *jihad*, to destroy the Mongol invaders of the Middle East in 1260, and to annihilate the crusader settlements, destroying their last stronghold of Acre in 1291.

But the main reason why Saladin and Hattin were for long forgotten was because, after the capture of Acre by the Mamluks in 1291, the cities of the Palestinian littoral were destroyed to prevent their being used as bases for invasion. This policy was highly successful in insulating the Middle East from western interference. Trade between Europe and Egypt continued, but it was channelled through Alexandria, and contact with the Christians, therefore, could be tightly controlled by the Mamluks. In the fourteenth century the Ottoman Turks based in Anatolia created an Islamic empire which seized Constantinople in 1453 and by the end of the sixteenth century had conquered Syria, Egypt, and Iraq, and extended their dominion over the Holy Places of Mecca and Medina. To the west the Ottomans conquered the Balkans and Hungary, and established their frontiers on the Adriatic Sea and eastern Austria. The Ottomans extended their power over the whole Middle East and threatened Europe itself. In these circumstances the crusades were largely forgotten, and with them Saladin and Hattin. This was not absolute. Majir al-Din al-Ulaymi (1456–1522) wrote a *History of Jerusalem* which provided a substantial and admiring picture of Saladin, while a seventeenth-century poem written at Jerusalem celebrates his memory in glowing terms, but both these works are concerned with the Holy Land where memory of the crusader incursion and expulsion could well have been fresher. However, by the time of Kaiser Wilhelm's visit in 1898 even Saladin's tomb at Damascus was neglected.

In the late nineteenth century the memory of the crusades, of Saladin and Hattin, was resurrected, and in a way that continues to influence modern politics. The impelling force was the recognition that a new Europe had established an enormous technological and industrial lead over the Islamic world and that this could no longer be held at bay. By then it was very evident that the Ottoman empire had ceased to be the bulwark of the *Dar al-Islam* against the *Dar al-Harb*, the 'House of War'. It was being stripped of its territories in the Balkans, its former North African provinces were seized by the French and Italians, while the British took over Cyprus and Egypt to protect their strategic lifeline to India, the Suez Canal. The Russian empire obviously wanted to seize Constantinople, and in 1878 was only stopped from doing so by concerted action by all the other European powers at the Berlin Congress.

The Ottomans reacted vigorously to this challenge, seeking to modernize their state and to reform its army even in the teeth of domestic opposition. But the threat, as they quickly realized, was multilayered. For with reform came ideological baggage. European nationalism infected the disparate peoples of the empire. The Christian Armenians, largely concentrated in the north-east of Anatolia, began to demand autonomy, even a nation of their own, and they could count on support from Russia. In time the Kurds to the south would raise similar demands. Moreover, from the late nineteenth century profound social and political changes were taking place in Arab society. As European trade and business expanded, a new middle class emerged in the urban centres. They were deeply discontented with Ottoman government, and powerfully struck by the prestige of the European states. As a result, long before the collapse of the Ottomans at the end of the First World War, a sense of Arab nationalism had emerged amongst this tiny urban elite.

One consequence of the western impact was the *Nahda*, a renaissance of Arab cultural life in the late nineteenth and early twentieth centuries which had the effect of enhancing political consciousness as well as fostering all kinds of knowledge. The native Christian groups in the Middle East had always maintained contact with Europe and they were especially influential in the *Nahda* because of their insight into what was happening in Europe. The first Arabic treatment of the crusades, a *History of the Holy Wars, Called the Wars of the Cross*, was produced in 1865 under the auspices of the patriarch of Jerusalem. It was only in 1899 that a general Muslim history, *Splendid Accounts in the Crusading Wars* by al-Hariri, appeared. Significantly, it was at this time that a distinctive Arab word for the crusades emerged. Even amongst the Turks themselves there was discontent. In 1872 a Turk, Malik Kemal, wrote a biography of Saladin based on Arabic sources. Significantly, Kemal was a member of the reform party, the Young Ottomans, which wanted to revitalize the empire by adopting European methods. They were driven into exile in Europe, but their ideas were followed by the Young Turks, who rose to power after 1908 as the Committee of Union and Progress, and eventually led the Ottoman empire into the First World War.

In these circumstances the Ottoman sultan Abdul al-Hamid (1876–1909), embittered by the loss of most of his European territories by the 1890s, turned to religion as the obvious cement for his failing empire. As European territories fell away, the empire had become ever more Islamic and in turn the sultan emphasized his role as caliph, spiritual leader of all the faithful. Even this was not without its problems, for the sultan's Sunni orthodoxy was not welcome to dissident Muslims, especially the Shi'ites, and did nothing to end the long-running revolt of the very puritanical Sunni Wahhabi sect in Arabia led by the house of Ibn Saud. However, one consequence of the Ottoman government's new attitudes was that within their lands there arose a sharp intolerance of other religions. In 1894–6 the Ottoman government raised *Hamidiye*, paramilitaries often recruited from the Kurds, who massacred Armenians, who in consequence appealed to nearby Russia for protection. As a result of all these pressures the sultan proclaimed that 'Europe is now carrying out a Crusade against us in the form of a political campaign', identifying the crusade of the past with modern imperialism and linking both with Sunni fundamentalism.[11] However, none of this saved Sultan Abdul al-Hamid who was deposed in 1909 by the Young Turk movement, the Committee of Union and Progress, against whom the last Ottoman Sultans were virtually powerless. The new regime in Constantinople was secular in outlook, sharing many of the ideas of the *Nahda*, but of course allied to a powerful Turkish nationalism.

Although the exponents of the Arab *Nahda* had little enthusiasm for the Ottomans, the crusader-imperialist linkage catered for the growing sense of victimhood across Islam and so became firmly embedded in their thought and added impetus to their exploration of the crusading past. They drew heavily on contemporary European writing about the crusades. Some British and French writers portrayed the crusading movement as a kind of 'muscular Christianity' foreshadowing modern imperialism. Others, notably Gibbon in his *Decline and Fall of the Roman Empire*, despised the raw fanaticism and attributed to crusaders motives of greed and opportunism. Combining these two attitudes gave the notion of crusader-imperialism a satisfactory intellectual underpinning. Arising out of this historical interest was a search for real Arab heroes, and not unnaturally this revived memories of Saladin, because it was he who had successfully led the fight against the crusaders, defeated the westerners at Hattin, and recovered the holy city of Jerusalem. And this city was a special flashpoint because under the influence of Zionism more and more Jews were emigrating from Europe to the Holy Land. Since they had long been treated with contempt in the Islamic world, their new prominence and wealth was viewed with special bitterness.

Resentment at the crusader-imperialism linkage was deepened by the outcome of the First World War when Britain and France divided up the Middle East between them, although the house of Ibn Saud was permitted to rule in what is now Saudi Arabia and a Hashemite prince governed in Jordan under British tutelage. Modern western opinion has all but forgotten the struggles which followed. French rule in Syria was contested in a series of revolts, while in 1932 Britain was forced to concede independence (albeit of a limited kind) to Iraq. In Palestine Arab revolts erupted in protest at both British rule and the increasing settlement of Jews, attracted by Zionist propaganda and the British promise of a Jewish homeland. During the long period of unrest which increased in bitterness in the early 1930s, the Palestinians celebrated Saladin and his victory at Hattin as encouragements. Indeed one of the annual commemorations used to enhance the sense of solidarity was held on 4 July, specifically to remember the victory of Hattin. One problem was that the mass of the Palestinian population lacked leadership because the local Arab elite, a handful of wealthy families, treated with the British but were primarily concerned to protect and extend their own spheres of influence. Symbolism was, therefore, particularly important as a source of cohesion, as was the sense of a religious war, a *jihad* against oppressors which, of course, could easily be linked in to the memory of Hattin. The turbulence in Palestine escalated, culminating in the sustained rebellion of 1936–9 during which some 5,000 Palestinians were killed in a savage repression by British troops. The course of the revolt was closely followed across the Arab world, most notably by the Muslim Brotherhood which had been established in Egypt in 1928 and spread rapidly into other Arab countries. This, of course, helped to spread the cult of Saladin and the memory of Hattin.

In the wake of the Second World War the European empires in the Middle East collapsed, though not without sharp conflict, because Britain and France both retained strategic interests in the area. In Palestine after 1945 waves of Jews arrived, fleeing from stricken Europe, and this resulted in a savage guerrilla war between Jews and Arabs which the British were unable to control. In consequence, the British withdrew from Palestine in 1948, precipitating a war between Jews and Palestinians backed by the Arab states of the area, which eventually led to the formation of the state of Israel and the expulsion of 700,000 Arabs into neighbouring territories. For these refugees Saladin and his victory at Hattin became a symbol of hope. The parallel between the Latin kingdom of Jerusalem and Israel, which occupied much the same territory, provided a permanent reminder of the crusading past. Israel came to be seen as a surrogate of the crusading impulse in the West and a continuation of imperialism by other methods. Events like the Anglo-French alliance with the Israelis to seize Suez in 1956 intensified belief in 'crusader-imperialism'. A 1958 biography of Saladin remarked:

> anyone reviewing the history of Saladin and his times will find that it reminds him of the events of our times. He appeared at a dark moment for the Muslim Middle eastern countries: weak and divided amongst themselves, they attracted the greed of their European enemies who snatched parts of their territory.[12]

It was no coincidence that when another biography, originally published in 1927, was reissued in 1958, it was given the new title *Saladin, the Hero Who Vanquished the West*.

After the Second World War secularism emerged as a dominant force in the Arab world as power became vested in middle-class elites for whom emulation of western models as a path to modernization was a central tenet. Some regimes were orientated to the US and others to the USSR, both of whom were European in tradition and encouraged secularism in their friends and allies. The rulers of these Arab states frequently looked back to the memory of Saladin and associated themselves with his name and deeds. In Iraq the dictator Saddam Hussein made much of the fact that he, like Saladin, came from Tikrit, and the province around it is called Saladin. In fact Saddam Hussein actually erected a statue of himself dressed as Saladin outside his gaudy Sajida Palace. Saddam was clearly portraying himself as the leader of the Arab people and heir of Saladin in his propaganda. The Third Armoured Division of the Iraqi army was given the title 'Saladin', which was deeply ironic given that Saladin was a Kurd and that the Iraqis brutally suppressed all Kurdish aspirations, even to the extent of using poison gas against them. In the lands around Israel Palestinian refugees banded together in the Palestine Liberation Organization (PLO) which named one of its fighting battalions 'Saladin' and another 'Hattin'. In so far as these states had a common focus it was pan-Arabism, the notion of a single Arab nation.

The most significant of these new Arab states appeared in Egypt in 1952 when a charismatic army officer, Gamel Abdel Nasser, led a revolution which overthrew King Farouk (1936–52), who was seen as an imperialist stooge, and established a republic whose president and effective dictator he became in 1956. It was no coincidence that the new republic adopted as its leading symbol the eagle of Saladin which later figured in the coats of arms of the Palestinians, of South Yemen, Libya, the Ba'ath Party, Iraq, and the United Arab Republic. Nasser's anti-imperialist stance made him immensely popular not only in Egypt but across the whole Arab world, and projected his message of secular pan-Arabism as the modernizing agency which would bring stability and respect to Arabs everywhere. In 1956, after he had national-ized the Suez Canal, Egypt was invaded by an alliance of Israel, France, and Britain whose real purpose was to destroy his regime. The failure of this invasion had many causes, not least US oppos-ition, but it was widely seen as a triumph for Nasser, and gave enormous impetus to his vision for the Arab peoples.

Nasser's regime beamed vigorous propaganda across the whole Middle East, and much of it clearly identified him with Saladin. The culmination of this material is the film *Al Nasser Salah ad-Din* (*Saladin the Victorious*), made in 1963. Its climax is the victory of Hattin and the subsequent capture of Jerusalem. Saladin is por-trayed as a flawless and noble leader by an actor who had at least a passing resemblance to the Egyptian dictator, and certainly the lines put in his mouth express the politician's ideas. 'My dream', he says at one stage, 'is to see the Arab nation united under one flag...hearts united and free of hate.'[13] Yet at the same time his stance is equalitarian and tolerant, reflecting Nasser's belief in Arab socialism, so that he even comforts humble crusaders who are portrayed as pawns of the selfish imperialism of their leaders. Saladin here serves as the perfect vehicle for the ideas and ambi-tions of Nasser. He exemplified the need for a strong leader who would bring the Arabs together once more, imbue them with self-confidence, crush Israel, and restore their position in the world. *Al Nasser Salah ad-Din* is certainly not the only Arab film about the crusades, but it is one of the most exciting.

Egypt was not the only secular regime in the Arab world to claim the heritage of Saladin. In 1947 the secularist Ba'ath party was founded, which became very influential in Syria and Iraq. In 1958, after only the briefest of negotiations and without any sustained study beforehand, Syria and Nasser's Egypt announced their merger in the United Arab Republic. On this occasion Nasser went to Saladin's tomb by the Grand Mosque in Damascus and pledged 'to follow Saladin's example to realize total Arab unity'.[14] However, the Syrians quickly realized that Egypt was the dominant party, and as a result the UAR collapsed in 1961. By 1966 the Syrian branch of the Ba'ath had separated abruptly from the Iraqi. As a result by 1970 Syria was a dictatorship under Hafez al-Assad while in Iraq Saddam Hussein was climbing to power. The dictatorship in Iraq was not alone in latching on to the glory of Saladin; so too did Syria. The military wing of the Ba'ath there, dominated by Hafez al-Assad, saw itself as the heart of the struggle against Israel and projected this in its propaganda. The most obvious invocation of the memory of Hattin and Saladin in Syria stands outside the citadel of the old city of Damascus. It is a massive bronze statue of Saladin on horseback in his moment of victory at Hattin. He is flanked on one side by a Sufi holy man and on the other by a simple foot soldier wielding a spear, while his horse tramples crusaders, including King Guy and Reynald of Châtillon. Its creator, Abdallah al-Sayed, claimed 'that the group represents Saladin not as an individual warlord but as leader who embodies a wave of popular feeling against the Franks'.[15]

Even the moderately conservative Jordanian monarchy has felt the need to associate itself with the victor of Hattin. At Kerak, the site of the great castle of Reynald of Châtillon, there is another equestrian statue of Saladin triumphant, and the fact that he clutches a cross in one hand suggests that this is a representation of his hour of victory at Hattin. Shortly after the Gulf War of 1991,

Sunni Muslims erected a statue of Saladin in Baghdad in an area which after the US invasion of 2003 became disputed between Sunni and Shi'ite. The statue was damaged in crossfire, and at one stage was 'transformed' into the Shi'ite warrior champion Ashtar. Of course statues recalling famous men and great events are unremarkable in the western world, but they are very much less common in Islamic countries, and these expensive and striking erections are indicative of Saladin's remarkable fame, his embodiment of Arab aspirations, and the anxiety of political forces to associate themselves with him.

One of the most significant organizations formed in the high tide of secular pan-Arabism was the PLO, established in 1964 by Arab states as a means of unifying the former Arab inhabitants of Israel who had fled into neighbouring countries. The PLO was never the only body claiming to represent the dispossessed, but it very quickly gained recognition in the Arab world which became increasingly focused on the struggle with Israel. The secularist approach of the PLO owed much to its concern to represent Christian Arabs, as well as the Muslims who formed most of its membership, and it was at pains to play down religious differences. After the 1967 Arab–Israeli War, in which Israel defeated Egypt, Jordan, Syria, and Iraq and vastly expanded its territories, the PLO reorganized itself and improved its military structure to carry on the struggle against Israel. By 1969 Yasser Arafat had become chairman of the powerful PLO Executive Committee, and because of his fiery oratory he was being hailed as a contemporary Saladin. The main PLO military force was made up of four brigades, all named after great Arab victories of the past. Amongst them was the Hattin Brigade which was stationed in Syria. Despite the glory of its name the brigade never joined battle during the 'Six Day War' of 1967. In September 1970 open conflict broke out between the PLO in Jordan and the Hashemite monarchy of that country—a conflict commonly referred to as 'Black September'. The Hattin Brigade failed to intervene and the PLO was crushed.

The secularist pan-Arabism of the leading states in the Arab world did not go without challenge for very long. Nasser's prestige was shaken by the defeat at the hands of Israel in the 'Six Day War' of 1967, and after his death in 1970 no comparable figure emerged to lead pan-Arabism. Deprived of its charismatic leader, the shortcomings in Arab secularism became very evident. The tiny elites which dominated the states of the Middle East were notoriously corrupt and self-seeking. For example, 74 per cent of the 23 million population of Syria is Sunni, but the regime is led by members of a sect which many Sunni do not recognize as Islamic, the Alawites. They, along with other Islamic sects and the Christians, dominate government and largely exclude the majority Sunni from power, wealth, and influence. The leadership of the PLO itself was increasingly seen as self-seeking, and increasingly outbid by radical groups, especially after they recognized the right of Israel to exist in 1993 and renounced violence and terrorism. Moreover the death of Yasser Arafat in 2004 created a void which has never been truly filled. The narrow self-interest of the elites of the Middle East became more and more obvious because of the workings of the global economy. The Middle East saw the same movement of populations to major cities as had occurred worldwide. There the poor and unemployed confronted corruption and the ostentatious wealth of its beneficiaries at close quarters, without any of the social support offered by traditional rural society. The hollowness of official anti-crusader rhetoric was all too obvious as the middle classes adopted western ways. At the same time education was spreading and the propaganda struggle within Arab societies sharpened, and along with it simple repression and governmental violence.

As a result, by the 1980s secularism with its creed of pan-Arabism faced much sharper challenges than ever before. In Iran an Islamic Revolution created the only Shi'ite state in the world, challenging both secularism and the world of the orthodox Sunni Muslims. In Egypt the Muslim Brotherhood, a deeply conservative religious movement established in 1928, was profoundly hostile to secularism. It spread quickly across the Middle East until it had a membership of some 2 million by the start of the Second World War. It was never able to combat the appeal of Nasser during his lifetime, but its simple slogan, 'Allah is our objective; the Koran is our law, the Prophet is our leader; Jihad is our way; and death for the sake of Allah is the highest of our aspirations', had enormous appeal in the new political situation in the wake of his death. And the Muslim Brotherhood was reinforced by the emergence of a more sophisticated and elaborated intellectual position constructed by the Egyptian Sayyid Qutb.

This deeply religious man spent the years 1948–50 in the USA where he conceived a hatred of secularism and all its works, which he regarded as western intrusions upon Islam. His experience of the US led him to condemn its society as *Jahiliyyah*, meaning literally chaos but with the special meaning of a word used to describe the state of pre-Islamic Arabia. For him the term 'crusade' covered all western influence in the life of Islam. Unlike the conservatives, Qutb preached the need for an active Islamic economic, social, and political life. The imprisonment and torture to which he was subjected before his execution for treason in

1966 simply deepened his hostility to the prevailing secularism. He and others demanded a return to the purity of Islam and the re-establishment of sharia law. Their writings exposed the limitations of pan-Arabism, for the Islam they proclaimed was all-embracing, universalist, and much more in the spirit of the Koran. In many ways their condemnation of the 'crusaders' carried more weight than that of the secularists because they truly saw crusades as religious wars in the fullest sense. Like Saladin and the Mamluks they were Sunni and desired not only to expel westerners, but also to purify the orthodox world by turning against the Shi'ites and all other dissidents. They offered only the barest Koranic toleration for Christians in their midst. This new radical Islam, with its bitter hatred of the crusader-imperialist West, quickly laid claim to the inheritance of Saladin and aspired to cleave a way to a new Hattin.

The rise of radical Islam was certainly not a unifying force. The erosion of secular pan-Arabism gave birth to a whole plethora of groups all claiming to represent the purity of religion. Some enjoyed sympathy from conservative Islamic regimes such as Saudi Arabia, but that state embraces Wahhabism, an Islamic sect with its own agenda. The radicals set the scene for a struggle for the heart and soul of Islam which rages to this day. This multifaceted conflict generated an enormous propaganda effort, but until the series of attacks culminating in 9/11 it attracted relatively little attention in the West. However, it was the unfolding of political events rather than simply theological sophistication which gave radical Islam its prominence.

Against this background, two explosions in Beirut on 23 October 1983 were highly significant. The US and France had formed an International Peacekeeping Force which established itself in

Lebanon to end the civil war there. However, Muslims saw this as intervention on behalf of the Christian Maronites and Israel. The suicide bombers targeted the French and US marine barracks, killing 58 French and 241 American servicemen. Hailed as a great victory over the US, not least because no retaliation followed, the success was attributed to a Shiʿite Lebanese group, Hezbollah, which was a notably radical fundamentalist formation. Afghanistan provided another success which contributed to the prestige of radical Islam. In 1979 the Soviet Union invaded Afghanistan in support of its client government, precipitating a powerful resistance which drew its strength from amongst Islamic devotees and radicals. The Soviet withdrawal in 1988 and the collapse of the regime in 1992 had many causes, not least the enormous foreign pressure exerted by the US, Pakistan, China, Saudi Arabia, Iran, and others who armed the rebels. But the people who did the actual fighting were perceived to be radical Muslims of the Afghan *mujahideen*, and they acquired enormous prestige in the Islamic world. The experience of success in Beirut and Afghanistan revealed that Muslims, and specifically radical Muslims, were not helpless before the might of great powers, although the price in human suffering, about 1 million civilian dead and massive displacements of populations in Afghanistan, was less noticed.

A key figure in the Afghan war was Osama bin Laden who rose to head a group called al-Qaeda (the Base). Like most of the other radicals he was deeply suspicious of the West, and after Saddam Hussein invaded Kuwait in 1990 and threatened Saudi Arabia, he demanded that the Saudi king drop his request for US military aid and rely instead on a legion of Arab fighters recruited by Osama bin Laden, on the grounds that only Muslims should fight to defend the two great shrines of Mecca and Medina. This was refused and Osama bin Laden then broke with the Saudis, deploring the presence of non-Islamic troops on the soil where once Muhammad had walked. In the name of his 'World Islamic Front for Crusade against Jews and Crusaders' he denounced all contact with the western powers and called for a war against them. The nature of the war was made crystal clear:

> This clearly indicates the nature of this war. This war is fundamentally religious. The people of the East are Muslims. They sympathized with Muslims against the people of the West, who are the crusaders.[16]

And he invoked the memory of Saladin and Hattin as the way forward to victory against the infidel:

> Salah-al-Din abided by the teaching of Islam and read the words of Almighty God. Thus he realized the way to break the disbelievers' might is by fighting in God's way.[17]

Osama bin Laden recurred constantly to the theme of crusader-imperialism and invoked the memory of Saladin, as in this excerpt encouraging resistance to the US in Iraq from a broadcast on Al Jazeera on 18 October 2003:

> This is the second message to our Muslim brothers in Iraq. O grandchildren of Sa'd, Al-Muthanna, Khalid, Al-Mu'anna, and Saladin [early Muslim commanders] May God's peace, mercy, and blessings be upon you. I greet you, your effort, and blessed Jihad. For you have massacred the enemy and brought joy to the hearts of Muslims, particularly the people of Palestine. May God reward you for that. You are to be thanked for your jihad. May God strengthen your positions and guide you to achieve your targets.[18]

Al-Qaeda is only one of many radical Islamicist groups. Hamas
(Enthusiasm), which controls the Gaza Strip, is an offshoot of the
Muslim Brotherhood. Although Islamic, it identifies the struggle
with Israel as political rather than religious. However it repeats
much the same kind of propaganda about crusader-imperialists
as others. Article 15 of its charter links Saladin's triumph at Hattin
with a widely believed and entirely false story about General
Allenby when his forces entered Jerusalem in 1917:

> There is no escape from introducing fundamental changes in educa-
> tional curricula in order to cleanse them from all vestiges of the
> ideological invasion which has been brought about by orientalists
> and missionaries. That invasion had begun overtaking this area follow-
> ing the defeat of the Crusader armies by Salah a-Din el Ayyubi [at
> Hattin]. The Crusaders had understood that they had no way to
> vanquish the Muslims unless they prepared the grounds for that with
> an ideological invasion which would confuse the thinking of Muslims,
> revile their heritage, discredit their ideals, to be followed by a military
> invasion. That was to be in preparation for the Imperialist invasion, as
> in fact [General] Allenby acknowledged it upon his entry to Jerusalem:
> 'Now, the Crusades are over.' General Gouraud stood on the tomb of
> Salah a-Din and declared: 'We have returned, O Salah-a-Din!'[19]

It is hardly surprising that the circumstances of the Palestinians
evoke particularly strong memories of Hattin. Thus a pro-
Palestinian website commemorates Hattin as a symbol of hope:

> This is the battle of Hattin, one of the most virtuous wars in the
> Islamic, and Palestinian history. The war ended with Salah Al-Deen
> Al-Ayobi kneeling to God thankfully, after putting down the cru-
> saders tent, and capturing their king...After the Hattin war the path
> was opened for the Muslims to free the rest of Palestine.[20]

Dr. ʿAbdullah Nasih ʿUlwan, professor of Koranic exegesis at King
Abdul Aziz University (Saudi Arabia) in the preface to his book,

*Salah Ad-din al-Ayyubi (Saladin): Hero of the Battle of Hattin,* explains why he chose Saladin and suggests lessons for the present day:

> When I show the present generation the secret of and reasons for victory at the Battle of Hittin, I draw the Muslim's attention to the right path in liberating Jerusalem from criminal Jews, unjust Zionism, and those who support them.[21]

But there is a plethora of radical Muslim movements, some of which believe in violence and some of which reject it or take an equivocal stance, and they all share the same crusader-imperialist stance and aspire to the inheritance of Saladin. Amongst these many make use of the memory of Hattin and advertise their concerns on the Internet. Thus one website, The Battles of Ramadan, explores Hattin and exhorts the reader, 'jihad is taking place in Syria, be part of it'.[22] Out of the chaos of Syria and weakness in Iraq a new and violent Sunni force has arisen. ISIS and its supporters also invoke the memory of Hattin. Authentictauheed.com recalls the battle of Hattin as an example for the whole Muslim world, argues that Saladin was the Osama bin Laden of crusaders, and praises him as the destroyer of the Shia who had permitted the crusaders and helped them.[23] A fierce supporter is Abdul Karim Hattin whose radicalism is sharply criticized on spittoon.org.[24]

The resonances of Hattin have spread far across Islam and they have not always played into the hands of the radicals. On a website composed of the 'Writings of an ordinary citizen who is deeply concerned about the sociopolitical conundrum in his beloved Malaysia', the story of Hattin is rehearsed at some length. The author draws some very broad and very moderate conclusions from the story, showing clearly that Saladin is not merely the creature of the radicals:

Eight centuries have passed since the time of Salahuddin's Islamic Union. Today's Muslims need an Islamic Union for the same reasons as they did back then. Although the Islamic world is not under attack by a coalition army, as it was at the time of the Crusades, it is facing many threats. Furthermore, the Islamic world has fallen behind other civilizations in terms of science, technology, culture, art, and thought. Ever since the nineteenth century, the Islamic world has been seriously harmed by the many false ideologies and philosophies produced elsewhere, imported into its midst by mis-guided people, and spread among those who were not familiar with the Qur'an's values. On the other hand, some radicals who claimed to represent Islam while doing their best to subvert its morality, often unknowingly helped those who were consciously sewing the seeds for later conflict.[25]

These statements all come from Sunni sources, because the Shi'ites have a quite different attitude to the memory of Hattin. Their attitude to Saladin, Hattin, and the crusader-imperialist dialectic is bound to be different because Saladin abolished the Fatimid (Shi'ite) caliphate of Cairo in 1171, and it has never been restored. In Iran the revolution of 1978–9 which overthrew the shah was the work of many groups, and much of the decisive fighting in 1979 was the work of the Marxist group, the People's Mujahedin of Iran. However, the driving force of the revolution was bitter resistance to the shah's attempt to modernize and secularize Iranian society, and contempt for the evident corrup-tion of his regime. This led to the establishment of an Islamic republic, the only Shi'ite state in the world, which is just as hostile to the West as any of the Sunni radicals. But it makes no appeal to the memory of Saladin or of his triumph at Hattin. For the Iranians and their close allies in Lebanon, Hezbollah (Party of God), Saladin was a persecutor and this obliterates the memory of Hattin. The memory of Saladin and of Hattin has become caught up in sectarian strife. In 1993 an Egyptian convert to Shi'ism condemned Saladin, entitling a chapter in his book 'Saladin: [the man who] Tolerated Crusaders and Oppressed Muslims'.[26] Others have followed suit, provoking a strong Sunni reaction, notably by Shakir Mustafa in his *Saladin: The Denigrated Holy Warrior and Pious King*. The tensions between Shi'ite and Sunni find expression on the Internet, notably in connection with the crusades. A website discussing Hattin proclaims, 'the Shiites allowed the crusaders to come into Palestine; the same way the Shiites allow the kuffar into Iraq; the Shia always betray the Muslims'.[27] In this way Saladin, who once appeared to be a unifying figure for the whole Islamic world, has become a symbol of the increasingly sharp division between Sunni and Shi'ite.

The Battle of Hattin had enormous consequences for Europe and the Middle East and its memory remains alive even to this day, sometimes in very odd ways. A report on consumer preferences in Zimbabwe, remarking on the marketing share of a detergent called 'Cold Power', remarked:

> The battle for brand supremacy for Cold Power [detergent] can be likened to the Battle of Hattin, on July 4, 1187, wherein Cold Power Africa Limited is as Saladin, and all competing brands are as The Kingdom of Jerusalem and its allies. The Kingdom of Jerusalem, weakened by internal disputes, was completely defeated at the Battle of Hattin on July 4, 1187.[28]

However, for people in the western democracies Hattin seems a distant event and their view of it is probably bound up with their general attitude to the crusades. The very word crusade has long been redolent of a crude fanaticism which is now something of the distant past, and is perhaps also associated with nineteenth-century imperialism which is regarded as equally shameful. At the same time the very word crusade still has overtones of self-denying idealism; it was no accident that *Crusade in Europe* was the title General Dwight D. Eisenhower gave to his own account of his period as Supreme Allied Commander against Hitler in 1944–5. There is a fundamental and long-standing ambivalence in the western attitude to crusading, so that the memory of Hattin has been tinged with regret at the failure of a bold experiment even amongst those who despise crusading. In recent years, and especially since 9/11, the memory of the crusades, of Saladin, and of Hattin has become more and more important. Radical Muslim groups seek to unite Islam by indentifying the West as the source of all its ills, and, therefore, preach hatred and direct action against it as a vital part of their struggle for the soul of Islam. The consequences of this development have shocked western populations. Many people in Europe and the US have been influenced by a persuasive book, *The Clash of Civilizations*, which promotes the theory that after the end of the Cold War between the West and the Soviet Union the most important source of conflict in the world will lie between peoples with different cultural and religious identities.[29] In this world view Hattin has a new relevance as an episode in a continuing struggle. This idea is given force by the proclamations of al-Qaeda and other radical bodies who look for violent confrontation and for whom Hattin is a symbol of hope, offering the promise of bloody triumph in the future. Indeed Osama bin Laden seemed to adopt Huntingdon's ideas enthusiastically as he spoke of his *jihad* against the alien civilization of the United States and its allies.

These ideas often pervade reporting of news events in the Middle East and elsewhere, and embody a generally simplified and hostile picture of Islam. They are in a curious way immensely strengthened by books and TV programmes conveying a deeply admiring picture of Islamic arts and architecture in which a view of Islam as infinitely superior to medieval Europe is promulgated. Art of the past implies a flowering left behind by time. This vision of a world polarized between cultural and religious blocks is deeply unhistorical, for many of mankind's nastiest wars have been fought within cultures. The worst conflicts before the cataclysms of the twentieth century were the wars of dynastic succession in China, while the most savage of the crusades was against heresy within Europe. Islam is not monolithic and radical Sunni groups who use Hattin as a rallying cry do not speak even for most Sunni, let alone the Shiʻites who they have so often persecuted. Hattin should not be remembered as a political slogan, but as a real event of considerable complexity.

Hattin arose out of bitter religious hatred, but to portray it simply as a battle between people inspired by religious hatred would be a caricature. Both King Guy of Jerusalem and Saladin were members of rival ruling military elites struggling with one another for domination in the Middle East. Guy needed to create a solid political base for his rule and saw victory as the way to achieve it and religious hatred as a spur to that end. Some of his followers were not merely sceptical of that end but quite prepared to deal pragmatically with Muslim leaders. Saladin was deeply ambitious, and as a member of a small, largely Turkish ruling class he knew that success in war would attract the loyalty of good soldiers eager for booty and that *jihad* would appeal to the leaders of Arab society, thereby making them acquiescent in arbitrary military rule and taxation. This course of action had many dangers, and above all it demanded success, which was why he was anxious to provoke the battle we call Hattin. On both sides there were those who feared the test of battle because they knew its outcome would be powerfully influenced by chance. We tend to see Hattin from the point of view of its outcome and to underestimate the influence of random factors. Had Saladin been killed or even badly injured by a crossbow bolt on 3 July, the result of the encounter would have been radically different. After all, at Hastings in 1066 Harold's death by an arrow, a chance factor, was the decisive moment in the battle.

Hattin was a great event which deserves to be studied for its own sake and not as a minor adjunct to some sweeping generalization like the 'Clash of Civilizations' which may be pervasive today but gone tomorrow. Saladin managed his army with great skill, and the outcome of Hattin made his reputation as one of the giants of history. Yet this was only one victory, and it did not bring the war to an end. In a sense Hattin was a wasted victory, and this perhaps explains why Saladin is not regarded as warmly in the Arab world as in the West.

This book is an attempt to look at a historical event and to explain how and why it happened. But we all have to face the current reality of the myth of Hattin, which has become a rallying cry for radical Islamic groups, and a factor in the politics of hate in the Middle East. It is as well to understand the depths of that hatred. Israel is its focus. It is a land of some 8 million people.[30] But many in the Middle East envisage their destruction, a new holocaust beyond even the achievement of Hitler and his minions. In the wake of his great victory Saladin was merciful to his defeated enemies, albeit for his own political reasons. There is little sense that the current ferment will throw up such a humanitarian figure.

# MAPS AND FIGURES

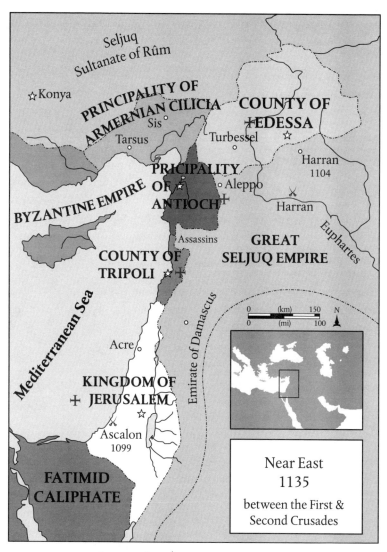

Map 1. The Crusader States at their greatest extent *c.*1135

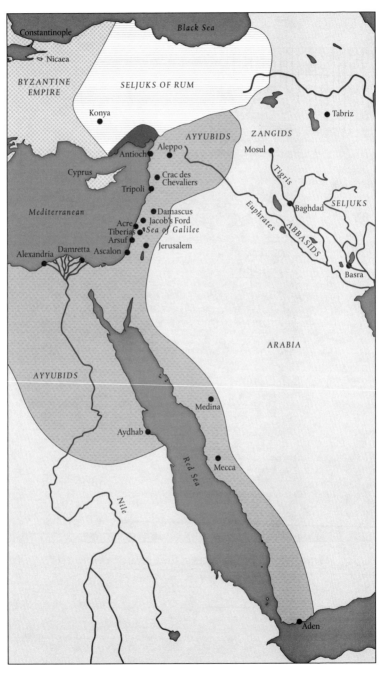

**Map 2.** The Empire of Saladin in 1190

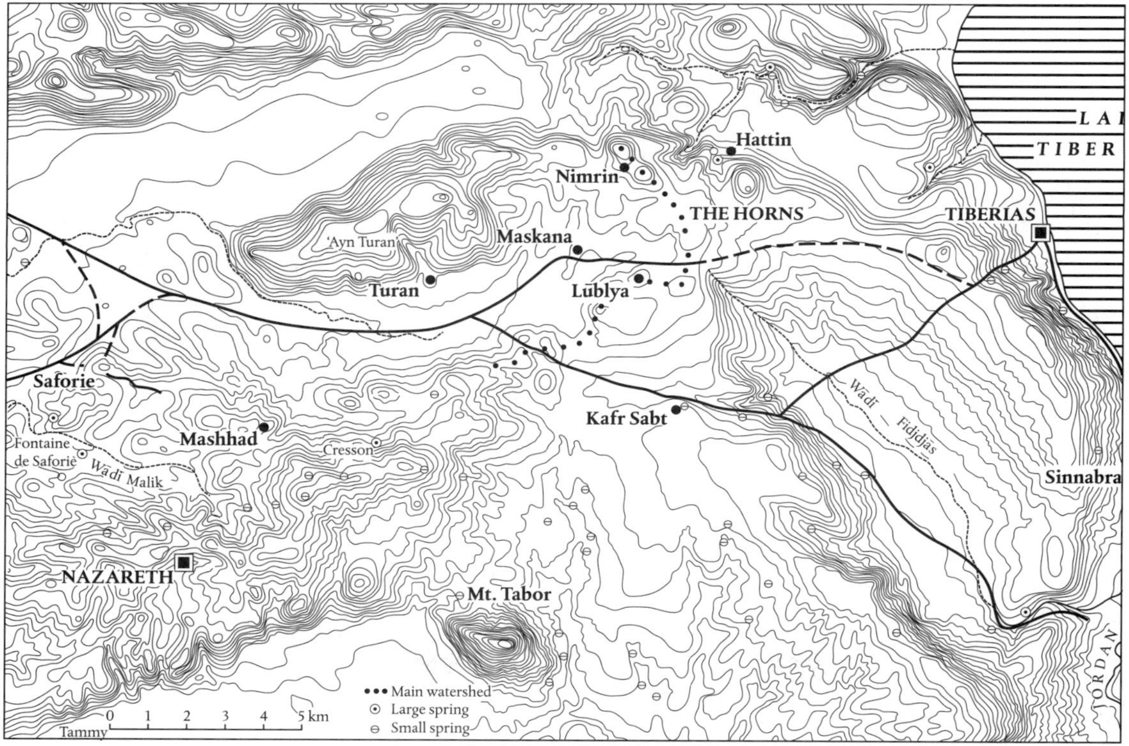

Map 3. The Battle of Hattin

173

**Figure 1.** The Edicule in the Church of the Holy Sepulchre

**Figure 2.** The Crusader Church of the Holy Sepulchre

**Figure 3.** Dome of the Rock or Mosque of Omar

**Figure 4.** Al-Aqsa Mosque

Figure 5. Antioch Citadel

Figure 6. Aleppo Citadel

Figure 7. Damascus Citadel

Figure 8. Acre, the Hospital Compound

**Figure 9.** Western Knights

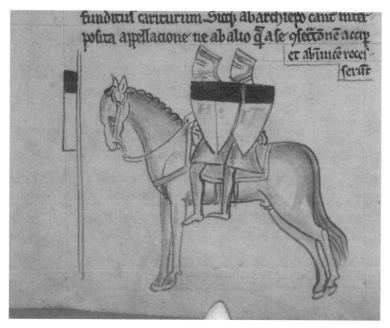

**Figure 10.** Two Templars on one horse, a symbol of humility and poverty

**Figure 11.** Turkish Horse Archer

**Figure 12.** Turkish Tribesmen

**Figure 13.** A battle between Crusaders and Muslims

**Figure 14.** The crossbow

**Figure 15.** Taking of Jerusalem in 1099 during the first crusade, from mid-14th century French edition of William of Tyre's *History of Deeds done beyond the Sea*

**Figure 16.** Saforie

**Figure 17.** Horns of Hattin

**Figure 18.** Hattin—the Gorge between the Horns

**Figure 19.** Saladin seizing the True Cross

Figure 20. Jerusalem Wall

Figure 21. Saladin and Richard jousting

**Figure 22.** Death of Saladin

**Figure 23.** Saladin Sculpture at Damascus

**Figure 24.** Eagle of Saladin as Egyptian coat of arms

**Figure 25.** Osama bin-Laden

**Figure 26.** 9/11: The Attack on the World Trade Centre

# NOTES

## Chapter 1

1. Imad ad-Din al-Isfahani, *Ciceronian Eloquence on the Conquest of the Holy City*, trans. in F. Gabrieli (ed.), *Arab Historians of the Crusades* (New York: Dorset Press, 1957), 135–6.

2. Raymond of Aguilers, *History of the Franks Who Captured Jerusalem*, trans. in A. C. Krey, *The First Crusade* (Gloucester, Mass.: Smith, 1958), 261.

3. C. D. Stanton, *Norman Naval Operations in the Mediterranean* (Woodbridge: Boydell, 2011), 20–1.

4. Bede, *History of the English Church and People*, trans. L. Sherley-Price and R. E. Latham (Harmondsworth: Penguin, 1955), 330, 347.

5. Trans. in J. D. Latham and W. Patterson, *Saracen Archery* (London: Holland Press, 1970), p. xxiii.

6. Augustine, Letter 153, trans. in O. O'Donovan and J. Lockwood, *From Irenaeus to Grotius: A Sourcebook in Christian Political Thought, 100–1625* (Grand Rapids, Mich.: Eerdmans, 1999), 125.

7. J. T. McNeill and H. M. Gamer, *Medieval Handbooks of Penance* (New York: Columbia, 1990), 224–5.

8. Rodulfus Glaber, *Histories*, ed. J. France (Oxford: Clarendon, 1989), 198–201.

9. Lambert, *Annals of Hersfeld*, 1065, in *Monumenta Germaniae Historica*, 3, ed. F. L. Barman (Berlin: MGH, 1905), 815–17.

10. Pope Urban II, *To the Church of Tarragona*, 1089, trans. in P. D. King (ed.), *Crusading and the Crusader States 1095–1192* (Cambridge: Cambridge Delegacy of Local Examinations, 1995), 9.

11. R. Somerville, *The Councils of Urban II*, i. *Decreta Claromontensia* (Amsterdam: Hakkert, 1972), 74.

12. Robert the Monk, *History of the First Crusade*, trans. C. Sweetenham (Aldershot: Ashgate, 2005), 79. The italicized section is from Psalm 78:8.

13. G. Duby, *The Three Orders: Feudal Society Imagined*, trans. A. Goldhammer of a French original of 1978 (Chicago: Chicago University Press, 1982), 40.

14. Ordericus Vitalis, *Historia Aecclesiastica*, ed. M. Chibnall, 6 vols (Oxford: Clarendon, 1969–79), iv. 287–96.

15. A. S. Tritton and H. A. R. Gibb, 'The First and Second Crusades from an Anonymous Syriac Chronicle', *Journal of the Royal Asiatic Society*, 2 (1933), 69.

16. *The Chronicle of Ibn al-Athir for the Crusading Period*, ii. 1146–1193, trans. D. S. Richards (Aldershot: Ashgate, 2007), 364.

## Chapter 2

1. Stephen of Blois, 'Second Letter to His Wife Adela, Spring 1098', trans. in Krey, *First Crusade*, 156. In this same letter, p. 131, Stephen told his wife he had been made 'lord and director and governor' of the army, so his statement about the Egyptian alliance must be regarded as authoritative.

2. Kemal ad-Din, *The Chronicle of Aleppo*, in *Recueil des historiens des croisades: Historiens occidentaux*, iii (Paris, 1866), 585–6. The *rais* of Aleppo, Boukat, son of Fares el-Fou'yi, was widely known as the Madman (*Moudjann*).

3. N. Christie and D. Gerish, *Preaching Holy War: Crusade and Jihad 1095–1105* (Aldershot: Ashgate Publishing, 2005).

4. Atabeg is a title given to one who governs on behalf of a minor. When the Seljuq Duqaq died in 1105 Tughtegin ruled on behalf of his heir—who in practice he ignored until they disappeared.

5. Kemal ad-Din, *The Chronicle of Aleppo*, 609.

6. William of Tyre, *Historia Rerum*, bk. 13, ch. 16, Eng. version in *A History of Deeds Done Beyond the Sea by William of Tyre*, trans. E. A. Babcock and A. C. Krey, 2 vols (New York: Columbia University Press, 1943), ii. 25. All further references will be to volume and page of this edition.

7. Jazira is the northern extension of the plain between the Tigris and Euphrates extending up into what is now Turkey.

8. Kemal ad-Din, *The Chronicle of Aleppo*, 614.

9. Kemal ad-Din, *The Chronicle of Aleppo*, 617, 618–19.

10. Walter the Chancellor, *The Antiochene Wars*, ed. T. Asbridge and S. B. Edgington (Aldershot: Ashgate, 1999), 161.

11. Trans. in C. Hillenbrand, 'Abominable Acts: The Career of Zengi', in J. Phillips and M. Hoch (eds), *The Second Crusade: Scope and Consequences* (Manchester: Manchester University Press, 2001), 111–32, at 124, 126–7.

12. *De Expugnatione Lyxbonensi*, trans. C. W. David (1936), ed. J. Phillips (New York: Columbia, 2001).
13. William of Tyre, *Historia Rerum*, ii. 192.
14. Ibn al-Qalanisi, *Damascus Chronicle of the Crusades*, trans. in Gabrieli (ed.), *Arab Chronicles of the Crusades*, 56–9.
15. Carl von Clausewitz, *On War*, ed. and trans. M. Howard and P. Paret (Princeton: Princeton University Press, 1976), 101.

## Chapter 3

1. William of Tyre, *Historia Rerum*, ii. 446.
2. William of Tyre, *Historia Rerum*, ii. 497.
3. Abu Shama, *The Book of the Two Gardens*, trans. in M. C. Lyons and D. E. P. Jackson, *Saladin: The Politics of the Holy War* (Cambridge: Cambridge University Press, 1982), 217.
4. *Chronique d'Ernoul and de Bernard le Trésorier*, ed. M. L. de Mas Latrie (Paris: Société de l'histoire de France, 1871). The distinguished medievalist R. H. C. Davies translated a part of this work as the *Chronicle of Ernoul* from Mas Latrie's text, but this has never been published and is held in Merton College Library MBV/ERN(1). The copyright holder is unknown. I should like to thank Merton library for having made it available to me. All further references to this text are to pages from the Mas Latrie edition as translated by Davies.
5. P. W. Edbury, *The Conquest of Jerusalem and the Third Crusade* (Aldershot: Ashgate, 1996) contains translations of all of the *Lyons Continuation* (pp. 11–145) and a small part of the *Colbert-Fontainbleau Continuation* (pp. 158–60) along with other sources. All further references to the *Continuations* will be to this edition.
6. Anonymous, *De Expugnatione Terrae Sanctae Libellus*, ed. J. Stevenson (London: RS 66, 1875), 221–2, trans. in J. A. Brundage (ed.), *The Crusades: A Documentary Survey* (Milwaukee, Wis.: Marquette University Press, 1962), 153–63. All further references to this text will be to the Brundage edition unless otherwise stated.
7. For an expanded view of these sources see the Bibliography, pp. 197–8.
8. *Lyons Continuation*, 46.
9. *Lyons Continuation*, 28.
10. *Lyons Continuation*, 26.
11. *Lyons Continuation*, 29.
12. Ibn al-Athir, *Chronicle*, ii. 321.

13. *Lyons Continuation*, 37.
14. *De Expugnatione Terrae Sanctae Libellus*, 155.
15. *De Expugnatione Terrae Sanctae Libellus*, 155–6.
16. *De Expugnatione Terrae Sanctae Libellus*, 155–6.
17. *Chronique d'Ernoul*, 162.
18. Ibn al-Athir, *Chronicle*, ii. 321.
19. *Colbert-Fontainebleau Continuation*, 159.
20. *De Expugnatione Terrae Sanctae Libellus*, 156.
21. *De Expugnatione Terrae Sanctae Libellus*, 156–7.
22. *Lyons Continuation*, 45.
23. *Lyons Continuation*, 45 and *Colbert-Fontainbleau Continuation*, 59; *Chronique d'Ernoul*, 169.
24. *Chronique d'Ernoul*, 167–8; *Lyons Continuation*, 45; *Colbert-Fontainbleau Continuation*, 159.
25. *De Expugnatione Terrae Sanctae Libellus*, 156.
26. *Chronique d'Ernoul*, 43.
27. We know nothing else about the knight John whose story is only told in a western manuscript Vatican Reg. Lat. 598; *Lyons Continuation*, 46.
28. *Lyons Continuation*, 47.
29. *Colbert-Fontainbleau Continuation*, 159.
30. *Chronique d'Ernoul*, 43–4.
31. *De Expugnatione Terrae Sanctae Libellus*, 158.
32. Terricus the Templar, *Letter*, trans. M. Barber, in *The New Knighthood* (Cambridge: Cambridge University Press, 1994), 115–16. A contemporary Genoese letter to the pope says that because they were penned in a 'rough and rocky place' they were 'unable to fight'.
33. Ibn al-Athir, *Chronicle*, ii. 322.
34. *De Expugnatione Terrae Sanctae Libellus*, 158.
35. Ibn al-Athir, *Chronicle*, ii. 322.
36. Ibn al-Athir, *Chronicle*, ii. 323.
37. Ibn al-Athir, *Chronicle*, ii. 323.
38. Ecclesiastes 10:16. Verse 16 in full reads: 'Woe to thee, O land, when thy King is a child, and thy princes eat in the morning. 17. Blessed art thou, O land, when they king is the son of nobles, and they princes eat in due season, for strength and not for drunkenness!' (King James Bible, 1611). After Hattin chronicles express a consensus that the defeat was God's punishment for the depravity of the kingdom.
39. *De Expugnatione Terrae Sanctae Libellus*, 156.
40. Ibn al-Athir, *Chronicle*, ii. 323.

## Chapter 4

1. P. K. Hitti, *Makers of Arab History* (London: Macmillan, 1968), 116.
2. Abu Shama, *Kitab al-rawdatayn*, in *Recueil des historiens des croisades: Historiens orientaux*, iv (Paris, 1898), 287.
3. Baha al-Din, *The Rare and Excellent History of Saladin*, trans. D. S. Richards (Aldershot: Ashgate, 2002), 74.
4. Ibn al-Athir, *Chronicle*, ii. 324.
5. Terricus the Templar, *Letter*, 115.
6. *Lyons Continuation*, 49.
7. *Lyons Continuation*, 55.
8. *Chronique d'Ernoul*, 50.
9. *De Expugnatione Terrae Sanctae Libellus*, 160.
10. *De Expugnatione Terrae Sanctae Libellus*, 161.
11. *De Expugnatione Terrae Sanctae Libellus*, 162. See the comments of P. J. Cole in 'Christian Perceptions of the Battle of Hattin', *Al-Masaq*, 6 (1993), 21–2.
12. *Lyons Continuation*, 62.
13. *Lyons Continuation*, 65.
14. It is nice to relate that William V was freed in 1188.
15. Ibn al-Athir, *Chronicle*, ii. 375.
16. Ibn al-Athir, *Chronicle*, ii. 375.
17. Baha al-Din, *History of Saladin*, 146.
18. Baha al-Din, *History of Saladin*, 165.
19. Baha al-Din, *History of Saladin*, 170–1.
20. Baha al-Din, *History of Saladin*, 168–70.
21. Baha al-Din, *History of Saladin*, 170.
22. Baha al-Din, *History of Saladin*, 175.
23. Ambroise, *The History of the Holy War*, ed. M. Ailes and M. Barber (Woodbridge: Boydell, 2003), 137.
24. H. J. Nicholson (ed.), *The Chronicle of the Third Crusade: A Translation of the Itinerarium Peregrinorum et Gesta Regis Ricardi* (Aldershot: Ashgate, 1997), 362.
25. Nicholson (ed.), *The Chronicle of the Third Crusade*, 368.

## Chapter 5

1. Chaucer, *Canterbury Tales*, General Prologue, l.72.
2. *De Expugnatione Terrae Sanctae Libellus*, 158–9.
3. *Lyons Continuation*, 57.

4. Anonymous, *Gesta Francorum et Aliorum Hierosolymitanorum*, ed. R. Hill (Edinburgh: Nelson, 1962), 21.

5. Ramon Lull, *Book of Knighthood and Chivalry of Raymond Lull*, ed. B. R. Price (includes anonymous *Ordene de chevalerie*) (Union City, Calif.: Chivalry Bookshelf, 2003), 108, 122.

6. Hitti, *Makers of Arab History*, 141.

7. For books on Saladin, see Bibliography, p. 202.

8. http://www.rumormillnews.com/cgi-bin/archive.cgi/noframes/read/ 33664, accessed 23 October 1013.

9. Dahlia Ravikovitch, *The Window: New and Selected Poems*, ed. and trans. C. Bloch and A. Bloch (New York: Sheep Meadow Press, 1989).

10. Trans. in Mohamed El-Moctar, 'Saladin in Sunni and Shi'a Memories', in N. Paul and S. Yeager, *Remembering the Crusades: Myth, Image and Identity* (Baltimore: Johns Hopkins, 2012), 199.

11. J. Riley-Smith, *The Crusades, Christianity and Islam* (New York: Columbia, 2008), 72.

12. Abd al-Munim Majid, quoted in E. Sivan, *Radical Islam: Medieval Theology and Modern Politics* (New Haven: Yale, 1990), 114.

13. P. B. Sturtevant, 'SaladiNasser', in N. Haydock and E. L. Risden (eds), *Hollywood in the Holy Land: Essays on Film Depictions of the Crusades* (Jefferson, NC: McFarland, 2009), 129.

14. T. Petra, *Syria* (London: Benn, 1972), 128.

15. C. Hillenbrand, *The Crusades: Islamic Perspectives* (Edinburgh: Edinburgh University Press, 1999), 600.

16. Osama bin Laden, 3 November 2001, accessed 8 October 2012 at http:// news.bbc.co.uk/1/hi/world/monitoring/media_reports/1636782.stm.

17. M. Scheuer, *Osama Bin Laden* (Oxford: Oxford University Press, 2011), 215 n. 105.

18. http://www.fas.org/irp/world/para/ubl-fbis.pdf, accessed 22 October 2013.

19. Hamas Charter (1988), http://www.thejerusalemfund.org/www. thejerusalemfund.org/carryover/documents/charter.html, accessed on 9 October 2012. In reality Allenby was careful not to mention crusading and he rebuked those who did, because much of his army consisted of Indian Muslims. The story about Gouraud equally has little foundation.

20. http://historyofpalestine.moonfruit.com/#/the-battle-of-hattin/ 4554085575, accessed 1 October 2012.

21. ʿAbdullah Nasih, *Salah Ad-din al-Ayyubi (Saladin): Hero of the Battle of Hattin*, trans. Khalifa Ezzat Abu Zeid (Dar al-Salam, Egypt) accessed on 1 October 2013 at http://kitaabun.com/shopping3/product_info.php?products_id= 262.

22. http://www.islamictube.com/watch/29810203/Muhammad-S-dr-1, accessed 22 October 2013.

23. Authentictauheed.com, accessed 29 October 2014.

24. Spittoon.org, accessed 2 October 2014.

25. http://alizul2.blogspot.co.uk/2011/08/ramadan-583-ah1187-ad-great-battle-of.html, accessed 1 October 2012.

26. Trans. El-Moctar, 'Saladin', 204–5.

27. http://www.authentictauheed.com/2011/08/battle-of-hattin-by-ustad-abu-nusaybah.html, accessed 23 October 2013.

28. http://www.thebehaviourreport.com/report/index.php/consumers/item/118-kuwachisana-wars, accessed 1 October 2013.

29. S. P. Huntingdon, *The Clash of Civilizations and the Remaking of World Order* (New York: Simon and Schuster, 1996).

30. *Jerusalem Post*, report by Danielle Ziri, 31 May 2013.

# BIBLIOGRAPHY

## I. Sources

### A. Christian

Anonymous, 'De Expugnatione Terrae Sanctae Libellus', ed. J. Stevenson (London: RS 66, 1875), 221–2, trans. in J. A. Brundage (ed.), *The Crusades: A Documentary Survey* (Milwaukee, Wis.: Marquette University Press, 1962), 153–63.

Barber, M., and Bate, K. (eds), *Letters from the East* (Aldershot: Ashgate, 2010).

*Chronique d'Ernoul et de Bernard le trésoirer*, ed. M. L. de Mas Latrie (Paris, 1871), 158–62.

Edbury, P. W. (ed.), *The Conquest of Jerusalem and the Third Crusade* (Aldershot: Ashgate, 1998); trans. of M. R. Morgan (ed.), *La Continuation de Guillaume de Tyr (1184–1197)* (Paris: Geunther, 1982).

'L'Estoire de Eracles Empereur', in *Recueil des historiens des croisades: Historiens occidentaux*, ii (Paris, 1859), 52–3.

Gerald of Wales, *The Journey through Wales and the Description of Wales*, ed. L. Thorpe (London: Penguin, 1978).

John of Ibelin, *Le Livre des assises*, ed. P. Edbury (Leiden: Brill, 2003).

Nicholson, H. J. (ed.), *The Chronicle of the Third Crusade: A Translation of the Itinerarium Peregrinorum et Gesta Regis Ricardi* (Aldershot: Ashgate, 1997).

Philip of Novara, *Le Livre de forme de plait*, ed. and trans. P. Edbury (Nicosia: Cyprus Research Centre, 2009).

*Rothelin Continuation of William of Tyre*, in *Recueil des historiens des crusades: Historiens occidentaux*, ii (Paris, 1859), 489–639; trans. J. Shirley in *Crusader Syria in the Thirteenth Century: The Rothelin Continuation of William of Tyre with Part of the Eracles or Acre Text* (Aldershot: Ashgate, 1999), 11–120.

Terricus the Templar, *Letter*, trans. M. Barber as *The New Knighthood* (Cambridge: Cambridge University Press, 1994), 115–16.

William of Tyre, *Historia Rerum in Partibus Transmarinis Gestarum*, ed. R. B. C. Huygens (Turnhout: Brepols, 1986); Eng. trans. in *A History of* the *Deeds Done Beyond the Sea*, ed. E. A. Babcock and A. C. Krey, 2 vols (New York: Columbia, 1943).

## B. Islamic

Abu Shama, *Kitab al-rawdatayn*, in *Recueil des historiens des croisades: Historiens orientaux*, iv (Paris, 1898), 286–7.

Ali al-Harawi, *Guide des lieux de pèlerinage*, ed. J. Sourdel-Thomine (Damascus: Institut Français, 1953).

Baha ad-Din Ibn Shaddad, *The Rare and Excellent History of Saladin*, trans. D. S. Richards (Aldershot: Ashgate, 2002).

Gabrieli, F. (ed.), *Arab Historians of the Crusades* (London: Routledge and Kegan Paul, 1969).

Hallam, E. (ed.), *Chronicles of the Crusades: Eye-Witness Accounts of the Wars Between Christianity and Islam* (London: Weidenfield and Nicolson, 1989), 157–60.

Hitti, P. K., *Makers of Arab History* (London: Macmillan, 1968).

Ibn al-Athir, *Chronicle of Ibn al-Athir for the Crusading Period*, trans. D. S. Richards, 3 vols (Aldershot: Ashgate, 2006–8).

Imad ad-Din al-Isfahani, *Ciceronian Eloquence on the Conquest of the Holy City*, trans. in F. Gabrieli (ed.), *Arab Historians of the Crusades* (New York: Dorset, 1957).

Kemal ad-Din, *The Chronicle of Aleppo*, in *Recueil des historiens des croisades: Historiens occidentaux*, iii (Paris, 1866), 577–655.

Melville, C. P., and Lyons, M. C., 'Saladin's "Hattin Letter"', in B. Z. Kedar (ed.), *The Horns of Hattin* (London: Variorum, 1992), 208–12.

## C. Source Studies

Abouali, D., 'Saladin's Legacy in the Middle East Before the 19th Century', *Crusades*, 10 (2011), 175–85.

Edbury, P. W., 'The Lyon *Eracles* and the Old French Continuations of William of Tyre', in B. Z. Kedar, J. Riley-Smith, and R. Hiestand (eds), *Montjoie: Studies in the Crusade History in Honour of Hans Eberhard Mayer* (Aldershot: Variorum, 1997), 139–53.

Edbury, P. W., *John of Ibelin and the Kingdom of Jerusalem* (Woodbridge: Boydell, 2003).

Edbury, P. W., and Rowe, J. G., *William of Tyre, Historian of the Latin East* (Cambridge: Cambridge University Press, 1988).

Gillingham, J., 'Roger of Howden on Crusade', in *Richard Coeur de Lion: Kingship, Chivalry and War in the Twelfth Century* (London, 1994), 147 [on Ernoul].

Morgan, M. R., *The Chronicle of Ernoul and the Continuation of William of Tyre* (London: Oxford University Press, 1973).

Pryor, J. H., 'The *Eracles* and William of Tyre: An Interim Report', in B. Z. Kedar (ed.), *The Horns of Hattin* (London: Variorum, 1992), 270–93.

## II. Secondary Works

### A. General Histories of Crusading

Jotischky, A., *Crusading and the Crusader States* (Harlow: Pearson, 2004).

Lewis, A. R., *Nomads and Crusaders 1000–1368* (Bloomington: Indiana University Press, 1988).

Mayer, H. E., *The Crusades*, trans. J. Gillingham (Oxford: Oxford University Press, 1972).

Richard, J., *The Crusades, c.1071–c.1291*, trans. J. Birrell (Cambridge: Cambridge University Press, 1999).

Riley-Smith, J., *The Crusades: A History* (London: Continuum, 2005).

Tyerman, C., *God's War: A New History of the Crusades* (Harvard, Mass.: Belknap, 2006).

### B. The Crusading States in the Twelfth Century

Angold, M., *The Byzantine Empire* (London: Longman, 1984).

Edbury, P. W., 'Looking Back on the Second Crusade: Some Late Twelfth-Century English Perspectives', in M. Gervers (ed.), *The Second Crusade and the Cistercians* (New York: St Martin's Press, 1992), 163–9.

Edbury, P. W., *John of Ibelin and the Kingdom of Jerusalem* (Woodbridge: Boydell Press, 1997).

Ellenblum, R., *Frankish Rural Settlement in the Latin Kingdom of Jerusalem* (Cambridge: Cambridge University Press, 1998).

Hamilton, B., *The Latin Church in the Crusader States: The Secular Church* (London: Variorum, 1980).

Hamilton, B., *The Leper King and His Heirs: Baldwin IV and the Crusader Kingdom of Jerusalem* (Cambridge: Cambridge University Press, 2000).

Harris, J., *Byzantium and the Crusades* (London: Hambledon, 2002).

Jubb, M., 'The Crusaders' Perceptions of Their Opponents', in H. J. Nicholson (ed.), *Palgrave Advances in the Crusades* (Basingstoke: Palgrave Macmillan, 2005), 225–44.

Lilie, R. J., *Byzantium and the Crusades* (Oxford: Clarendon, 1994) (Eng. trans. of *Byzanz und die Kreuzfahrstaaten* (Munich, 1981)).

Mayer, H. E., 'The Latin East, 1098–1205', in D. Luscombe and J. Riley-Smith (eds), *The New Cambridge Medieval History*, vol. iv. *c.1024–c.1198*, pt. ii (Cambridge University Press, Cambridge 2004), 644–74.

Murray, A. V., *The Crusader Kingdom of Jerusalem: A Dynastic History 1099–1125* (Oxford: Unit for Prosopographical Research, 2000).

Neocleous, S., 'Byzantium and Saladin: Opponents of the Third Crusade?', *Crusades*, 9 (2010), 87–106.

Phillips, J., 'The Latin East, 1098–1291', in J. Riley-Smith (ed.), *The Oxford Illustrated History of the Crusades* (Oxford: Oxford University Press, 1995), 112–40.

Phillips, J., *Defenders of the Holy Land: Relations Between the Latin East and the West, 1119–1187* (Oxford: Clarendon Press, 1996).

Prawer, J., *Histoire du royaume latin de Jérusalem*, 2 vols (Paris: Centre national de la recherche scientifique, 1969–70).

Prawer, J., *The Latin Kingdom of Jerusalem* (London: Weidenfeld and Nicholson, 1972).

Riley-Smith, J., 'Peace Never Established: The Case of the Kingdom of Jerusalem', *Transactions of the Royal Historical Society*, 5/28 (1978), 87–102.

Riley-Smith, J., 'The Crusades, 1095–1198', in D. Luscombe and J. Riley-Smith (eds), *The New Cambridge Medieval History*, vol. iv. *c.1024–c.1198*, pt. ii (Cambridge University Press, Cambridge 2004), 534–63.

Smail, R. C., 'Latin Syria and the West, 1149–1187', *Transactions of the Royal Historical Society*, 5/19 (1969), 1–20.

### C. Islam and the Crusades

Dajani-Shakeel, H., 'Al Quds: Jerusalem in the Consciousness of the Counter-Crusader', in V. P. Goss (ed.), *The Meeting of Two Worlds: Cultural Exchange Between East and West During the Period of the Crusades* (Kalamazoo, Mich.: Medieval Institute Publications, 1986), 201–21.

Elisséeff, N., 'The Reaction of the Syrian Muslims After the Foundation of the First Latin Kingdom of Jerusalem', in M. Shatzmiller (ed.), *Crusaders and Muslims in Twelfth Century Syria* (Leiden: Brill, 1993), 162–72.

Hillenbrand, C., *The Crusades: Islamic Perspectives* (Edinburgh: Edinburgh University Press, 1999).

Holt, P. M., *The Age of the Crusades* (Harlow: Longman, 1986).

Irwin, R., 'Islam and the Crusades, 1096–1699', in J. Riley-Smith (ed.), *The Oxford Illustrated History of the Crusades* (Oxford: Oxford University Press, 1995), 217–59.

Kedar, B. Z., 'The Subjected Muslims of the Frankish Levant', in J. M. Powell (ed.), *Muslims under Latin Rule* (Princeton: Princeton University Press, 1990), 135–74.

Moosa, M., 'The Crusades: An Eastern Perspective, with Emphasis on Syriac Sources', *Muslim World*, 93 (2003), 249–89.

Richards, D. S., ''Imād al-Dīn al-Isfahānī: Administrator, Litterateur and Historian', in M. Shatzmiller (ed.), *Crusaders and Muslims in Twelfth-Century Syria* (Leiden: Brill, 1993), 133–46.

Shatzmiller, M., 'New Directions in the Study of Islam and the Crusades', *Scripta Mediterranea*, 25 (2005), 73–6.

### D. European Warfare

Contamine, P., *War in the Middle Ages*, trans. M. Jones (Oxford: Blackwell, 1984).

France, J., *Western Warfare in the Age of the Crusades, 1000–1300* (London: University College London Press, 1999).

France, J., 'Recent Writing on Medieval Warfare: From the Fall of Rome to c.1300', *Journal of Military History*, 65/2 (2000), 441–73.

Gillingham, J., 'Richard I and the Science of War in the Middle Ages', in Gillingham and J. C. Holt (eds), *War and Government in the Middle Ages: Essays in Honour of J. O. Prestwich* (Woodbridge: Boydell Press, 1984), 78–91.

Gillingham, J., 'William the Bastard at War', in C. Harper-Bill et al. (eds), *Studies in Medieval History Presented to R. Allen Brown* (Woodbridge: Boydell Press, 1989), 141–58.

Verbruggen, J. F., *The Art of Warfare in Western Europe During the Middle Ages: From the Eighth Century to 1340*, trans. S. Willard and R. W. Southern (Woodbridge: Boydell, 1997).

### E. Crusading Warfare

Bennett, M., 'The Crusaders' "Fighting March" Revisited', *War in History*, 8 (2001), 1–18.

Edbury, P. W., 'Feudal Obligations in the Latin East', *Byzantion*, 47 (1977), 328–56.

Edbury, P. W., 'Warfare in the Latin East', in M. Keen (ed.), *Medieval Warfare: A History* (Oxford: Oxford University Press, 1999), 89–112.

Ellenblum, R., 'Frontier Activities: The Transformation of a Muslim Sacred Site into the Frankish Castle of Vadum Jacob', *Crusades*, 2 (2003), 83–98.

France, J., 'Crusading Warfare and Its Adaptation to Eastern Conditions in the Twelfth Century', *Mediterranean Historical Review*, 15/2 (2000), 49–66.

France, J., 'Crusading Warfare', in H. J. Nicholson (ed.), *Palgrave Advances in the Crusades* (Basingstoke: Palgrave Macmillan, 2005), 58–80.

Hamilton, B., 'The Elephant of Christ, Reynald of Châtillon', *Studies in Church History*, 15 (1978), 97–108.

Richard, J., 'Les Listes de seigneuries dans le livre de Jean d'Ibelin', *Revue historique de droit français et étranger*, 32 (1954), 565–77.

Smail, R. C., *Crusading Warfare, 1097–1193* (1972; 2nd edn, Cambridge: Cambridge University Press, 1995).

### F. Islamic Warfare

Eddé, A.-M., *Saladin*, trans. J. M. Todd (Cambridge, Mass.: Harvard University Press, 2011) (Fr. orig., Paris: Flammarion, 2008).

Ehrenkreutz, A. S., *Saladin* (Albany, NY: State University of New York Press, 1972).

Guard, T., 'Military Service, Careerism and Crusade', *Chivalry, Kingship and Crusade*, 38 (2013), 123–43.

Hamblin, W. J., 'Saladin and Muslim Military Theory', in B. Z. Kedar (ed.), *The Horns of Hattin* (London: Variorum, 1992), 228–38.

Humphreys, S., 'Zengids, Ayyubids and Seljuqs', in D. Luscombe and J. Riley-Smith (eds), *The New Cambridge Medieval History*, vol. iv. c.1024–c.1198, pt. ii (Cambridge: Cambridge University Press, 2004), 721–52.

Lyons, M. C., and Jackson, D. E. P., *Saladin: The Politics of the Holy War* (Cambridge: Cambridge, University Press, 1982).

Möhring, H., *Saladin: The Sultan and His Times, 1138–1193* (Baltimore: Johns Hopkins University Press, 2008).

Shatzmiller, M., 'The Crusades and Islamic Warfare—A Re-Evaluation', *Der Islam*, 69/2 (1992), 247–87.

Stevenson, W. B., *The Crusaders in the East: A Brief History of the Wars of Islam with the Latins in Syria during the Twelfth and Thirteenth Centuries* (Cambridge: Cambridge, University Press, 1907).

### G. The Military and Political Background to Hattin

Baldwin, M. W., *Raymond III of Tripolis and the Fall of Jerusalem* (Princeton: Princeton University Press, 1936).

Barber, M., 'Frontier Warfare in the Latin Kingdom of Jerusalem: The Campaign of Jacob's Ford, 1178–1179', in J. France and W. G. Zajac (eds),

*The Crusades and Their Sources: Essays Presented to Bernard Hamilton* (Aldershot: Ashgate, 1998), 9–22.

Edbury, P. W., 'Propaganda and Faction in the Kingdom of Jerusalem: The Background to Hattin', in M. Shatzmiller (ed.), *Crusaders and Muslims in Twelfth Century Syria* (Leiden: Brill, 1992), 173–89.

Lyons, M. C., and Jackson, D. E. P., *Saladin: The Politics of the Holy War* (Cambridge: Cambridge University Press, 1982).

Nicholson, R. L., *Joscelyn III and the Fall of the Crusader States* (Leiden: Brill, 1973).

Pringle, D., *The Churches of the Crusader Kingdom of Jerusalem*, ii (Cambridge: Cambridge University Press, 1998), 351–66 [description of Tiberias].

Pringle, D., 'The Spring of Cresson in Crusading History', in M. Balard, B. Z. Kedar, and J. Riley-Smith (eds), *Gesta Dei per Francos: Études sur les croisades dédiées a Jean Richard* (Aldershot, 2001), 231–40.

Smail, R. C., 'The Predicaments of Guy of Lusignan, 1183–1187', in B. Z. Kedar, H. E. Mayer, and R. C. Smail (eds), *Outremer: Studies in the History of the Crusading Kingdom of Jerusalem Presented to Joshua Prawer* (Jerusalem: Yad Izhak Ben-Zvi Institute, 1982), 159–76.

### H. Hattin

Barber, M., 'The Battle of Hattin and Its Consequences', in Barber, *The Crusader States* (New Haven: Yale University Press, 2012), 289–323.

Cole, P. J., 'Christian Perceptions of the Battle of Hattin (583/1187)', *Al-Masaq*, 6 (1993), 9–39.

DeVries, K., 'The Battle of Hattin, 1187: Beginning of the End', *Medieval History Magazine*, 5 (2004), 24–31.

Ehrlich, M., 'The Battle of Hattin: A Chronicle of a Defeat Foretold?', *Journal of Medieval Military History*, 5 (2007), 16–32.

Herde, P., 'Die Kämpfe bei den Hörnen von Hittin und der Untergang des Kreuzritterheers', *Römische Quartalschrift für christliche und Altertumskunde unnd Kirchengeschichte*, 61 (1966), 1–50; rev. version in Herde's *Studien zur Papst- und Reichsgeschichte: Gesammelte Abhandlungen und Aufsätze*, ii/1 (Stuttgart: Hiersemann, 2002), 97–152 (reviewed in English by B. Kedar, *Crusades*, 7 (2008), 291–3).

Hoch, M., 'Falken, Tauben und der Elefant Gottes: Hattin, 4 Juli 1187', in S. Förster et al., *Schlachten der Weltgeschichte: Von Salamis bis Sinai* (Munich: Beck, 2003), 79–92, 398–9.

Hoch, M., 'Battle of Hattin (1187)', in A. V. Murray (ed.), *The Crusades: An Encyclopedia*, 4 vols (Santa Barbara, Calif.: ABC Clio, 2006), ii. 559–61.

Housley, N., 'Saladin's Triumph Over The Crusader States: The Battle of Hattin, 1187', *History Today*, 37/7 (1987), 17–23.

Kedar, B. Z., 'The Battle of Hattin Revisited', in Kedar (ed.), *The Horns of Hattin* (London: Variorum, 1992), 190–207.

Nicolle, D., *Hattin 1187: Saladin's Greatest Victory* (London: Osprey, 1983).

Prawer, J., 'The Battle of Hattin', in Prawer, *Crusader Institutions* (Oxford: Clarendon Press, 1980), 484–500.

Richard, J., 'An Account of the Battle of Hattin Referring to the Frankish Mercenaries in Oriental Muslim States', *Speculum*, 27/2 (1952), 168–77.

Smail, R. C., 'The Predicaments of Guy of Lusignan,' in B. Z. Kedar et al., *Outremer* (London: Variorum, 1982), 168–9.

Sourdel-Thomine, J., 'Les Conseils du Shaikh al-Harawi à un Prince Ayyubide', *Bulletin d'études orientales*, 17 (1961–2), 205–66 [visited shrines of areas perhaps as a spy].

### I. Holy War and Jihad

Cole, P. J., '"O God, The Heathen Have Come Into Your Inheritance" (Ps. 78.1): The Theme of Religious Pollution in Crusade Documents, 1095–1188', in M. Shatzmiller (ed.), *Crusaders and Muslims in Twelfth-Century Syria* (Leiden: Brill, 1993), 84–111.

Gerish, D., 'The True Cross and the Kings of Jerusalem', *Haskins Society Journal*, 8 (1996), 137–55.

Gilchrist, J., 'The Papacy and War Against the "Saracens", 795–1216', *International History Review*, 10 (1988), 74–97.

Gilchrist, J., 'The Lord's War as the Proving Ground of Faith: Pope Innocent III and the Propagation of Violence (1198–1216)', in M. Shatzmiller (ed.), *Crusaders and Muslims in Twelfth-Century Syria* (Leiden: Brill, 1993), 65–83.

Katzir, Y., 'The Conquests of Jerusalem, 1099 and 1187: Historical Memory and Religious Typology', in V. P. Goss (ed.), *The Meeting of Two Worlds: Cultural Exchange Between East and West During the Period of the Crusades* (Kalamazoo, Mich.: Medieval Institute, 1986), 103–13.

Ligato, G., 'The Political Meanings of the Relic of the Holy Cross among the Crusaders and in the Latin Kingdom of Jerusalem: An Example of 1185', in M. Balard (ed.), *Autour de la Première Croisade* (Paris: Publications de la Sorbonne, 1996), 315–30.

Murray, A. V., '"Mighty Against the Enemies of Christ": The Relic of the True Cross in the Armies of the Kingdom of Jerusalem', in J. France and W. G. Zajac (eds), *The Crusades and Their Sources: Essays Presented to Bernard Hamilton* (Aldershot: Ashgate, 1998), 217–38.

Partner, P., 'Holy War, Crusade and *Jihad*: An Attempt to Define Some Problems', in M. Balard (ed.), *Autour de la Première Croisade* (Paris: Publications de la Sorbonne, 1996), 333–43.

Siberry, E., *Criticism of Crusading, 1095–1274* (Oxford: Clarendon Press, 1985).

Smalley, B., *The Study of the Bible in the Middle Ages* (Oxford: Blackwell, 1952).

## J. Historiography

Chevedden, P. E., 'The Islamic View and the Christian View of the Crusades: A New Synthesis', *History*, 93/2 (2008), 181–200.

Cole, P. J., 'Christian Perceptions of the Battle of Hattin (583/1187)', *Al-Masaq*, 6 (1993), 9–39.

Curtis, M., *Orientalism and Islam: European Thinkers on Orientalism in the Middle East and India* (New York: Cambridge University Press, 2009).

El-Moctar, Mohamed, 'Saladin in Sunni and Shiʿ[ra1] a Memories', in N. Paul and S. Yeager (eds), *Remembering the Crusades: Myth, Image and Identity* (Baltimore: Johns Hopkins, 2012), 197–214.

Ellenblum, R., *Crusader Castles and Modern Histories* (Cambridge: Cambridge University Press, 2007).

Housley, N., *Contesting the Crusades* (Oxford: Blackwell, 2006).

Jubb, M., *The Legend of Saladin in Western Literature* (New York and Lampeter: Mellen Press, 2000).

Riley-Smith, J., 'History, the Crusades and the Latin East, 1095–1204: A Personal View', in M. Shatzmiller (ed.), *Crusaders and Muslims in Twelfth-Century Syria* (Leiden: Brill, 1993), 1–17.

Riley-Smith, J., 'The Crusading Movement and Historians', in Riley-Smith (ed.), *The Oxford Illustrated History of the Crusades* (Oxford: Oxford University Press, 1995), 1–12.

Singh, N. K., and Samiuddin, A. (eds), *Encyclopaedic Historiography of the Muslim World* (Delhi: Global Vision, 2003).

Sivan, E., *Radical Islam: Medieval Theology and Modern Politics* (New Haven: Yale, 1990).

# PICTURE ACKNOWLEDGEMENTS

23. © Robert Hillenbrand
24. By Mohamednajm (Own work) [Public domain], via Wikimedia Commons
25. © Alamy / World History Archive
26. © Getty Images / Spencer Platt

# INDEX